Take Cover, Spokane

A History of Backyard Bunkers, Basement Hideaways, and Public Fallout Shelters of the Cold War

By Lee O'Connor

Contents

Introduction

I don't remember the Realtor or the former owner mentioning ANYTHING about a bomb shelter on the property—not a word.

—Pia K. Hansen

Spokesman-Review reporter Pia K. Hansen was astonished when she stumbled upon a mysterious hole in the ground in 2004. She discovered a tree stump in the outdoor patio floor of her Spokane, Washington, home hid an entrance to a Cold War shelter that had been buried under the backyard by a previous owner and forgotten. Her friends gave her a list of possible uses for the space: "wine cellar, an art studio, an underground hangout, even a pool." In 2005, Hansen declared that she had not hit upon the right idea of how to utilize the backyard bunker space and had sealed the entrance for safety's sake. In the headline of the story she wrote about her shelter, she asked, "How many huge holes are in back yards across Spokane?" Her question leads to an exploration of the history of Spokane's backyard bunkers, basement hideaways, and public fallout shelters of the Cold War.[1]

I. Shelter Mania

Now, in the thermonuclear age, any misjudgment on either side about the intentions of the other could rain more devastation in several hours than has been wrought in all the wars of human history.

—President John F. Kennedy

Everything will be swell as long as there is no World War III. But in that event, heaven help us!

—Spokanite Gottfried S. Ehrenberg

Take cover, Spokane, Washington. That thought propelled residents into a fallout shelter mania in the summer and fall of 1961. "It soon reached the point," Spokane humorist Kent Graybill recalled, "where if you weren't at least planning a shelter in the basement or under the petunia bed, you were practically un-American." Years earlier, Soviet leader Nikita Khrushchev had bellowed at the capitalist countries, "We will bury you!" In the midst of Spokane's obsession with shelter digging, Spokanite Mrs. June G. Potter observed, "Maybe Khrushchev won't have to 'bury us' after all—we seem to be doing it for him."[2]

People living in Spokane and the rest of the United States took an interest in fallout shelters that was described by political commentators in Washington, D.C., as a "mania" after President Kennedy delivered his Berlin Crisis speech on July 25, 1961. On radio and television, the President told the public that he would use diplomacy and, if necessary, risk nuclear war to combat Soviet attempts to push United States forces out of West Berlin. Along with highlighting a possible path toward Armageddon, Kennedy's Berlin Crisis speech addressed civil defense. He explained, "In the event of an attack, the lives of those families which are not hit in a nuclear blast and fire can still be saved—if they can be warned to take shelter and if that shelter is available." Toward that end, Kennedy declared his intention to ask Congress for funds "to identify and mark space in existing structures—public and private—that could be used for fall-out shelters in case of attack; to stock those shelters with food, water, first aid kits and other minimum essentials for survival." After proposing a public fallout shelter program, Kennedy added, "In the coming months, I hope to let every citizen know what steps he can take without delay to protect his family in case of attack," which many in the United States interpreted as a nod to do-it-yourself backyard bunker and basement hideaway builders.[3]

Two months before the Berlin Crisis address, Kennedy had made a speech to Congress setting America's sights on the moon, but in contemplation of a possible war with the Soviet Union, he led the nation underground. Spokane followed.[4]

Unlike tornado-prone parts of the United States, Spokane had only one reason to adopt shelters: the threat of nuclear war. Spokane city officials viewed their city as a potential target of nuclear attack as early as 1950, when Spokane Superintendent of Schools John A. Shaw declared, "The same thing that happened to Hiroshima and Nagasaki could happen here, and we must prepare for it." The Federal Civil Defense Administration (F.C.D.A.) affirmed Shaw's concern when it named Spokane one of 271 potential targets of atomic attack in the United States in 1951. The F.C.D.A. kept Spokane's target status "Restricted" information until 1953. Upon receiving the news September 18, 1953, that the F.C.D.A. had declassified its targeting predictions, Carl D. Canwell, the City of Spokane's public safety commissioner and civil defense administrator, said he was "glad that they've decided to tell the people the truth. For a long time I've known that we are sitting on an atomic bomb pile."[5]

Spokane likely made the F.C.D.A. roster of potential targets of Soviet attack because the city had a large population (from 1940 to 1960, the number of residents grew from 122,000 to 181,600), was a railroad hub, and possessed an industrial base that had demonstrated its worth to the military during World War II. More than anything, however, the presence of U.S. Air Force bombers and missiles increased the Spokane area's chances of attracting destruction. In 1951, B-36 Peacemaker bombers moved into Fairchild Air Force Base, twelve miles west of Spokane, and remained until 1956 when B-52 Stratofortress bombers arrived at the base. The B-52s remained until 1994. The Air Force stationed nine Atlas E nuclear-tipped ICBMs in nine bases scattered north, south, east, and west of Spokane from April 1, 1960, to June 25, 1965. At least two of the missile bases were fewer than twenty-five miles from the city. The B-52 bombers, one of which was christened *City of Spokane*, and the Atlas missiles, one of which was dubbed *Spirit of the Inland Empire*, were all capable of delivering nuclear strikes to the Soviet Union. With the addition of the Atlas missile sites, Spokanite Gottfried S. Ehrenberg predicted in a letter to the *Spokesman-Review* that the Soviets would be "marking Spokane with a red pin on their military maps as a priority target." While only the Soviets knew for certain whether Spokane and the nearby military sites were actually targets, and how many warheads were actually directed at these areas, it is reasonable to presume that the city was in the atomic cross-hairs and that the Spokane region would have been heavily hit by nuclear weapons in the event of a war.[6]

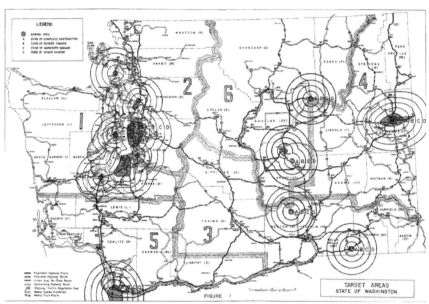

Figure 1   **The Washington State Civil Defense Department estimated that the Puget Sound area faced a wider swath of destruction than Spokane, but Spokane was likelier to be hit in the lead attack. Washington State Civil Defense Director Charles C. Ralls predicted to Bill Newman of the *Seattle Times* on August 19, 1960: "Missile bases and perhaps long-range bomber bases in eastern Washington, would be among logical, first enemy targets." On March 15, 1962, Ralls mailed a copy of this "Target Areas" map to a Denver resident who wanted to know how safe Washington would be in a nuclear war. (Washington State Archives, State Government Archives, Olympia. Hereafter referred to as WSA, SGA, Olympia)**

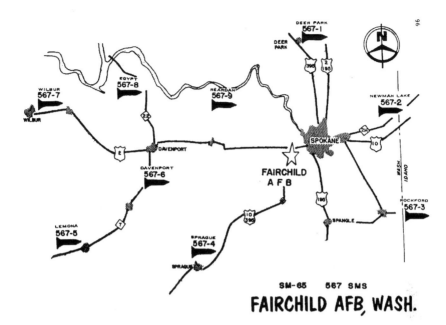

FAIRCHILD AFB, WASH.

Figure 2   At the height of shelter mania in the early-1960s, the Spokane area hosted nine Atlas missile bases, and B-52 bomber planes were stationed at Fairchild AFB. The missiles and planes could all carry nuclear payloads and attack the Soviet Union. (www.siloworld.com)

United States Air Force General Curtis Lemay told members of Congress in 1960 that the Soviet Union would have to launch "between 10 and 30" Soviet missiles to destroy a hardened U.S. missile base. The nine Atlas E missile sites around the Spokane area were partially buried, semi-hardened, coffin-style silos that had 25 percent of the protection from blast pressures enjoyed by hardened missile sites located fully underground. If the Soviets had hit the Atlas E bases with a quarter of the arsenal Lemay estimated they would need to strike at hardened bases, then by the SAC commander's reckoning, the Spokane region sat in the eye of a storm that could have been composed of twenty-three to sixty-eight nuclear warheads—on top of however many bombs the

Soviets would deploy to lash out at the B-52s stationed at Fairchild AFB and in addition to whatever the Soviets might or might not have thrown at Spokane.[7]

Obviously, the Spokane area would have been an attractive target to the Soviet military planners who made decisions about which targets to strike in the event of a nuclear war. The question was, could Soviet weapons reach Spokane? Yes. During the Cold War, the Soviet Union developed the capability to deliver nuclear warheads to targets in the United States via airplane, missile, and submarine. In the lead-up to the shelter mania in 1961, Spokanites learned of the possible threat of Soviet airplanes and missiles flying towards Spokane from over the North Pole. On October 14, 1953, the North Central High School auditorium rang with the words of Brig. Gen. T. Alan Bennett, the commander of the 25th Air Division at McChord Air Force Base. Bennett addressed Spokane's volunteer plane-spotting group. He cautioned the audience to "remember that enemy atomic bomber bases (over the north pole) are just as close to Spokane as is New York city." In support of 1957's Operation Alert civil defense drill, George Cheek, a staff writer for the *Spokesman-Review*, published a story that imagined what it would be like if Spokane were subject to a nuclear attack. In Cheek's scenario, "Spokane was one of the first to be struck. The bombs swept in over the north pole, far above the earth's surface, moving at fantastic speeds. There were warnings at places farther from the pole, but the bomb that exploded high above the intersection of Sprague and Washington was unexpected. Suddenly it was there."[8]

Did the Soviets have enough weapons to target Spokane without compromising their ability to strike at Washington, D.C., or at gigantic population centers like New York? Yes, eventually.

Figure 3   **Spokane knew that it was close to Soviet bases located within striking distance of the city by a quick-flight across the North Pole. This map appeared in *Spokane: Your Civil Defense Manual*, a creation of Spokane and Spokane County civil defense groups in collaboration with American Radio Publications. The manual was undated but probably appeared around 1956. Hereafter referred to as *Spokane: Your Civil Defense Manual*, 1956. (Author's Collection)**

Since the end of the Cold War, historians have learned that the Soviet Union was far behind the United States in nuclear weapons production during the 1950s and early 1960s. Although the Soviets possessed nuclear weapons that were comparable in number and strength to United States weapons by 1969, in 1962 they had only enough bombers and missiles to fly 300 nuclear warheads to the United States while the United States could strike at the Soviet Union with 3,000 nuclear weapons they could deliver by plane and 327 missiles armed with nuclear warheads.[9]

At the time of the shelter mania in 1961, the United States public did not know the Soviets were so poor in nuclear weapons. In fact, the 1957 Soviet launch of the Earth's first artificial satellite, Sputnik, had led the United States public to fear it was falling behind the Soviets in rocket development. A 1960 Gallup Poll showed that during the Kennedy-Nixon election campaign about half the United States believed in a missile gap that favored the Soviet Union. At a hand-shaking stop in Spokane, Kennedy warned an audience, "We have fallen behind the Soviet Union in the development and production of ballistic missiles—both intercontinental and those of intermediate range." Shelter mania operated on the assumption that Kennedy was right.[10]

Even if the Soviets had directed only a single nuclear bomb or missile at Spokane, it would have been at least as devastating as the city's great fire of August 4, 1889, that wrecked downtown and caused J. H. Boyd, an eye-witness to the fire's aftermath, to write: "It is enough to break almost anybody's heart to see the terrible destruction of our beautiful city—every noble brick and stone building that once looked so fine and handsome layed [sic] in dust and ashes. In fact every way we turn there appears to be nothing but desolation." During a civil defense drill on April 26, 1954, that included a make-believe attack on Spokane by a single 50-kiloton atomic bomb detonated over downtown, Spokane Civil Defense Director John J. Lenhart told the press, "Had a bomb actually exploded over Spokane today, the queen city of the Inland Empire now would be a desert of rubble. The downtown district would look as if some giant bulldozer had swept across it, leaving in its wake smoldering stones, broken bricks and chunks of steel." An unidentified "team of atomic explosion experts," consulted by Lenhart's department, determined that if the hypothetical bomb had been real it would have destroyed 5.725 square miles of the city, killed 8,000 people, injured 24,000, and left 42,000 homeless.

On March 19, 1955, U.S. Navy Commander Jack D. Dean told a group of Washington State's civil defense leaders at a conference at the Davenport Hotel that, after an atomic attack against Spokane, the survivors would need to dig a trench six feet wide and fourteen miles long to bury the dead.[11]

The Soviet Union's development of incredibly powerful hydrogen bombs made the apparent threat of an attack on Spokane even graver. The Soviets test-fired their first H-bomb in 1953 and then went on to break the bounds of all previous arms tests in 1961, when Khrushchev's scientists set off a thermonuclear super bomb. The blast, equal to 50 megatons of dynamite, was the largest human-made explosion in the history of the world. Even though Spokane Civil Defense Director Clyde Friend cast doubt on the possibility that the Soviets could ever use such a large bomb in battle—he said it was "of little military value" and declared it merely a "psychological weapon"—he could not stop people from wondering what would happen if the super bomb hit town. The *Spokane Daily Chronicle* quizzed Friend on this topic and reported to its readers that if Spokane were struck by a 50-megaton nuclear weapon, "the area of total death and destruction of all but the best reinforced concrete buildings would extend at least 14 miles from the city center, embracing almost all of Spokane County, except north of Denison and south of Spangle." Of course, even if the Soviets were not ready to roll out their super bomb for use in the field, they could still destroy the Spokane area with much of the same effect as the super bomb's, by employing multiple, smaller-sized, nuclear weapons. In March 1962, the Washington State Civil Defense Department underscored Spokane's vulnerability to any type of nuclear attack by distributing a map of "principal targets" in Washington State that labeled all of Spokane and most of Spokane County as a "zone of complete destruction."[12]

Figure 4 In 1950, the *Spokesman-Review* pegged downtown Spokane for "total destruction" in a nuclear war. The paper also admonished: "For scoffers who consider Spokane an unimportant target it is interesting to note that this community, along with the Puget Sound area and the Columbia basin, are the closest points to known air bases in Russian Siberia, a flight of six hours." (*Spokesman-Review*)

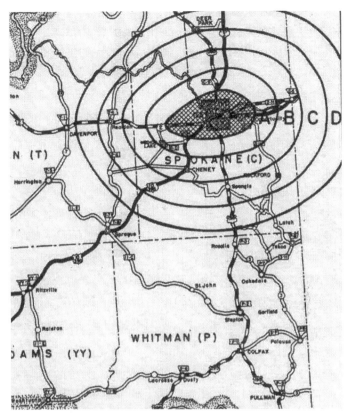

Figure 5   In 1962, the Wash. State Civil Defense Dept.
predicted that the entire City of Spokane would
be in a "zone of complete destruction," indicated
by the "A" circle. The cross-hatched area shows
the enemy's "aiming area." (WSA, SGA, Olympia)

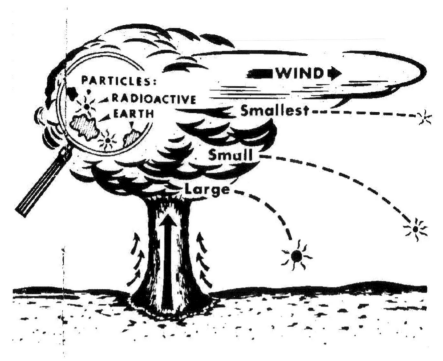

Figure 6   "Exposure to this 'fallout'," Spokane area civil
defense officials warned, "could cause reactions
in humans ranging from minor sickness to death.
On the other hand, persons who seek protection
inside 'fallout shelters' will face little or a greatly
reduced hazard. . . . It is possible that you could
safely leave the shelter in 2 to 14 days after
detonation." (Spokane City Plan Commission and
U.S. Army Corps of Engineers, *Community
Shelter Plan for Spokane and Spokane County*)

The point that Spokane would not fare well in a nuclear attack was not lost on Spokane writer Kent Graybill. He likely epitomized the thoughts of many in the region when he expressed his view in 1962 that "no shelter of any kind would be any protection within miles of a prime target area like Spokane."

Given that there was a great, and well-publicized, chance that a Soviet nuclear attack against the United States would destroy Spokane, why did anyone in the area turn to shelters? If the Soviet Union somehow missed Spokane, then shelters might have saved lives by shielding people from fallout, radioactive showers of pulverized dirt and debris, that would have landed on the city from nuclear blasts that occurred upwind of the region. Fallout protection would have been useful because victims of the nuclear bombings of Hiroshima and Nagasaki show that fallout causes symptoms that can range from slight nausea to a horrific, drawn-out, painful death, depending on the exposure.[13]

A 1958 federal civil defense booklet warned, if fallout from a mushroom cloud drifted down to earth it could "make you seriously ill even if the radioactive particles do not settle on you. It could kill you!" To be more specific, human health is threatened by three components of fallout: alpha and beta particles and gamma rays. Civil defense planners were mostly concerned about the gamma rays. A U.S. Office of Civil and Defense Mobilization publication aimed at executives overseeing shelter surveys explained: "Alpha and beta emitters may be dangerous if they are ingested through contaminated food, water, or air, but from the shelter standpoint they present no problem. Alpha particles cannot penetrate the external layer of skin, and beta particles cannot penetrate heavy clothing. However, *gamma rays, like X-rays, are highly penetrating,* and can cause serious damage to living tissue. *The primary aim of fallout shelter is to provide a shield against gamma radiation* [emphasis in original]."[14]

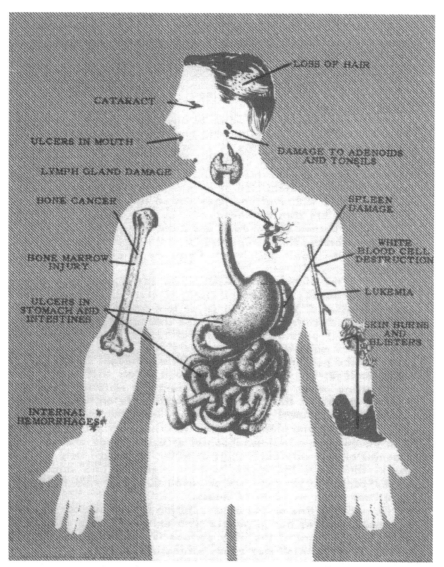

Figure 7   If a fallout shelter were unavailable, or poor, there could be terrible consequences, as demonstrated by "What Radiation Can Do," an illustration, borrowed from *Life* magazine that appeared in *Spokane: Your Civil Defense Manual*, 1956. (Author's Collection)

Civil defense officials measured the gamma radiation–shielding abilities of earth and various construction materials and used that information to survey buildings and determine the factor to which they could protect occupants from fallout. A protection factor (PF) of 100 meant that a shelter occupant would receive 100 times less radiation than a person standing outside the shelter under the open sky. The U.S. Office of Civil and Defense Mobilization found that PFs could range widely: underground shelters with three feet of earth cover, 1,000 PF or greater; basement fallout shelters in heavy masonry residences, 250 to 1,000; and basement fallout shelters in frame and brick veneer residences, 50 to 250. Even if a building wasn't designed or modified to be a shelter, it could still offer significant protection factors: subbasements of multistory buildings and underground installations (mines and tunnels), 1,000 or greater; basements without exposed walls and the central areas of tall buildings constructed with thick materials, 250 to 1,000; and central areas of basements with exposed walls and the central areas of the upper floors in buildings of heavy-duty construction, 50 to 250. The lowest protection factors were offered by basements without exposed walls in one or two-story buildings and the central areas of upper floors in multistory buildings of light construction, 10 to 50 PF; partially exposed basements in one or two-story buildings and central areas on ground floors of heavily constructed buildings, 2 to 10; and aboveground areas of wood houses, 2 or less.[15]

According to Spokane Civil Defense Director Clyde H. Friend, most Spokane area public fallout shelters had protection factors of 100 or greater. Based on figures from the OCDM, private shelters in backyard bunkers and basement hideaways would have offered the same degree of protection or better. Was 100 PF enough protection? In 1956, the US Government would have said no. At that time, it set the minimum federally approved protection factor at 1,000. In 1960, the government's answer would have been that the shelters were perfectly adequate because that year it dropped the minimum protection factor to 100. The government would have rated the shelters in Spokane even higher when it slashed the minimum protection factor to 40 during the Cuban Missile Crisis in 1962.[16]

Despite the fact that the federal government's minimum protection factors appeared to be arbitrarily handicapped, Spokane region civil defense officials assured the public that they could beat fallout. Friend and other Spokane civil defense leaders said that Spokanites would probably survive a nuclear war if they stayed in shelters for two weeks. On November 14, 1963, City of Spokane Civil Defense Assistant-Director Weymeth C. McGrew promised, "A large majority of Spokane area residents would survive a nuclear attack if they had adequate fallout protection." On September 1, 1961, Friend coached residents, "It is possible occupants would not have to remain two weeks, but the shelter should be stocked with that idea in mind."[17]

Figure 8   Backyard bunker. Spokane civil defense leaders
were initially short on details when they
recommended shelters in the 1950s. The drawing
above was accompanied by brief instructions
that "such a shelter can be constructed of wood,
concrete, concrete block, cattle passes, silos, or
steel tanks. When less massive materials are
used, the earth covering should be deeper." The
illustration appeared in Spokane: *Your Civil
Defense Manual*, 1956. (Author's Collection)

Figure 9　Basement hideaway. Spokane civil defense leaders said "basement shelter is better" because "radiation danger here is about one-tenth of the out-of-doors count." *Spokane: Your Civil Defense Manual*, 1956. (Author's Collection)

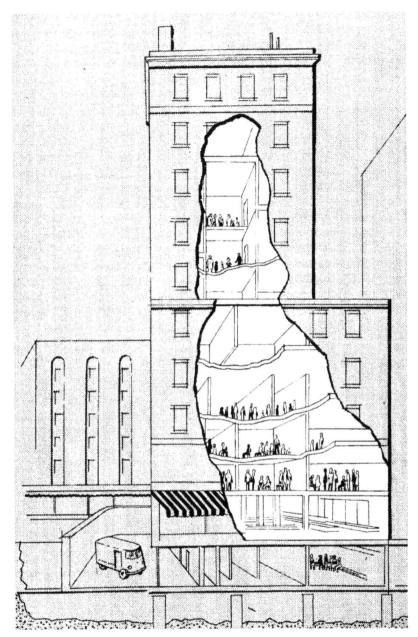

Figure 10   **Public fallout shelter. This illustration of shelter areas in the central core and basement of a building appeared in *Personal and Family Survival*—a manual of the federal Office of Civil Defense—in 1966. (Author's Collection)**

Civil defense planners based their survival predictions on the premise that Spokane would receive a light amount of fallout, but the fallout levels in Spokane in the event of a nuclear war would likely have been severely high. As the federal government dropped its minimum protection factor dramatically, the Soviet Union was testing nuclear weapons capable of yielding increasing amounts of fallout. Also, Spokane's position downwind approximately 150 miles northeast from the Hanford Atomic Bomb Works added to the fallout threat. Atomic Energy Commission scientists had calculated in a secret report in 1948 that the City of Spokane would be included in a potential "hazard area" in the event of a reactor accident at Hanford. If the entire Hanford complex, including its reactors and waste storage tanks, were bombed in the event of a nuclear war, the hazard to the City of Spokane, and other areas downwind of Hanford, would have been much greater than the danger posed by a lone reactor accident. In May 1956, the Washington State Civil Defense Department issued a bulletin that included information about "radioactive waste contained in storage tanks in the Hanford area." The bulletin relayed word from scientific authorities "that this material, when sucked up by a megaton surface burst, could create a destructive area far in excess of anything that has been calculated to date."[18]

Spokane's vulnerability to fallout caught the attention of scientist James E. McDonald of Arizona. In 1959, he cited Spokane as a particularly ill-fortuned city because of its close proximity to Atlas ICBM installations. In a letter to the *Spokane Daily Chronicle*, the scientist from the University of Arizona's Institute of Atmospheric Physics singled out the Spokane region's nine Atlas missile bases, then under construction, "as possibly the most astonishing of all" the ICBM bases across the United States. A majority of the Spokane area bases were upwind of Spokane, and if the sites were hit with Soviet nuclear weapons, then the fallout that resulted would inundate city residents with lethal amounts of radioactivity.

While McDonald fretted over missile bases, Spokane's *Spokesman-Review* celebrated "Mi$$ile" bases. The newspaper heralded the arrival of the Atlas as a potential economic boom, calling it an "Intercontinental Ballistic Mi$$ile" and claiming it was "bound to have a stimulating effect upon the local economy," assuring readers that "this proposed installation should add greatly to our own security, both local and national." McDonald's letter indicated that the Atlas missile bases, profitable or not, would actually jeopardize Spokane's security. To create a debate, the *Spokane Daily Chronicle* solicited an expert opinion on the matter from Washington State Democratic Senator Henry M. Jackson, presumably expecting that Jackson would provide a rebuttal to McDonald's concern. Sen. Jackson, a noted anti-communist and war hawk dubbed "the congressional spokesman for the military-industrial complex" for his championing of new weapons systems, made an interesting response, which could not exactly be called a rebuttal. Jackson did not deny the risk that the missile bases posed to Spokane. As a member of the Senate Armed Services Committee and the Joint Committee on Atomic Energy, he understood perfectly that the city was in danger. "Assuming a missile with an atomic warhead was aimed from more than 5,000 miles away to one of the missile bases near Spokane," Jackson figured, "a variation of 20 to 30 miles is very possible and the bomb could explode in the heart of the city anyway." In Jackson's view, why fret about the risk of fallout from destroyed missile bases upwind of Spokane when Soviet targeting was so unreliable that Spokane faced the potential of destruction from a direct hit by an errant warhead.[19]

Jackson's less-than-reassuring answer to McDonald's concern about the risk of fallout illustrated the unpredictable and frightening variables posed by the threat of nuclear war with the Soviet Union. Considering the grave picture painted by the Senator, it is tempting to wonder if people were in their right minds when civil defense officials convinced them to spend money to build private fallout shelters or to expend volunteer effort to establish public fallout shelters. In essence, people who adopted the fallout shelter concept were hoping that Soviet weapons might not reach Spokane and trusting that Kennedy might have been right in his Berlin Crisis speech when he said, "In the event of an attack, the lives of those families which are not hit in a nuclear blast and fire can still be saved—if they can be warned to take shelter and if that shelter is available." They were encouraged in this line of wishful thinking by civil defense leaders. Spokane Civil Defense Director Friend told a reporter on October 30, 1961, "The city is not a prime target." Operating within the bounds of that assumption, he rejected the idea that a fallout shelter was a waste. Instead, he labeled it "the best single-premium insurance which is possible to buy." Hundreds of Spokane residents bought that insurance.[20]

A spokesperson from the Spokane Civil Defense Department estimated that city residents had built approximately 300 private shelters in the backyards and basements of their homes by 1967. By 1969, the year that NASA astronauts fulfilled Kennedy's challenge to the nation to land a man on the moon, Spokane area property owners had cooperated with civil defense authorities to establish public fallout shelters stocked with survival supplies in the basements and densely shielded sections of 249 buildings in Spokane and Spokane County. In 1971, Spokane Civil Defense Director Lloyd F. Bloomington boasted that there were enough private and public fallout shelters in Spokane area businesses and residences to protect all 283,077 citizens of the City of Spokane and Spokane County.[21]

And, this wasn't the first time that people in the Spokane area turned to shelters. Duck-and-cover moments in the Spokane region date back to the Indian Wars.

II. Shelters in the Indian Wars, 1858, 1877

Colonel Wright smote the Indians with the A-bomb of the day.

—The Rainbow Seekers

The superpower showdown that produced the fallout shelter phenomenon of the twentieth century had similarities with the territory struggles that brought fighting to the Spokane region in the nineteenth century and inspired soldiers, Indians, and settlers to seek shelter. The link between the Cold War and the Indian Wars was never more strangely highlighted than it was on April 17, 1961, when Air Force Colonel T. S. Jeffrey, Jr., was escorting an Atlas intercontinental ballistic missile from Fairchild Air Force Base, through the freshly decommissioned George Wright AFB, to a launch base outside the City of Spokane, following a path similar to the route U.S. Army Colonel George Wright had led his troops along during his 1858 campaign against the region's Indians—a route, as Wright described it in his own words, "marked by slaughter and destruction." At the Idaho border, Colonel Jeffrey's missile party was met by descendants of Chief Garry of the Spokane Indians, a legendary figure who had faced Colonel Wright to negotiate peace. According to a Fairchild AFB newspaper account of the missile meeting, Garry's great-grandson, Ignace H. Garry, and Ignace's son, Joseph Garry, notable Indian leaders in their own right, welcomed the missile party. Any words that Colonel Jeffrey and the Garrys might have exchanged went unrecorded in the base newspaper, but Colonel Jeffrey had remarked on the Atlas missile's relation to the Spokane region's Indian history at an earlier event.[22]

At a March 29, 1961, ceremony held at the recently closed George Wright AFB—where 1961's "Miss Spokane" pageant winner Sally Ann Amick broke a bottle of champagne over a trailer carrying an Atlas missile dubbed the *Spirit of the Inland Empire*—Colonel Jeffrey had told the crowd that the "ground on which we stand was the scene of local Indian uprisings in which Col. George Wright played an important part in insuring the gates of the Northwest were kept ajar." Colonel Jeffrey continued:

> Today we stand on the same ground with a weapon before us that is far above the dreams of the early soldier. No longer are we posed for local trouble areas alone. This weapon, although it is our sincere desire that it never be fired, is capable of dealing a swift blow half way around the world. Such is our deterrent posture today.[23]

Colonel Jeffrey's glowing portrayal of Colonel Wright was distorted in casting Wright as a defender rather than an invader, but he showed a clear tie between the Cold War and the Indian Wars.

On May 6, 1858, Lieutenant Colonel Edward J. Steptoe led a U.S. Army reconnaissance mission out of Fort Walla Walla and headed north to investigate the Spokane and Palouse Indians, who were upset about white encroachment in their territory. Approximately thirty-five miles south of the present-day site of the City of Spokane, Colonel Steptoe's party was met and defeated by a coalition of Spokane, Palouse, Couer d' Alene, and Yakama

Figure 11 **Champagne sprayed wildly when Sally Ann Amick christened an Atlas missile called the *Spirit of the Inland Empire*, on March 29, 1961. At the ceremony, Colonel Jeffrey praised Colonel Wright for his brutal 1858 campaign against Indians in the Spokane area. Jeffrey added, "Today we stand on the same ground with a weapon before us that is far above the dreams of the early soldier." (*Fairchild Times*)**

Indians, along with members of other tribes. In the fight, Steptoe's soldiers dug shelters that essayist Randall A. Johnson described as "shallow firing pits" to shield themselves from the Indians' weapons, which included guns, bows and arrows, and lances.[24]

When U.S. Army Colonel George Wright marched his forces to the vicinity of Steptoe's defeat—with orders from his superior to "attack all the hostile Indians you may meet, with vigor; make their punishment severe, and persevere until the submission of all is complete"—he gave Spokane area Indians cause to improvise shelters of their own.

Figure 12   **During an April 17, 1961, journey to install an Atlas intercontinental ballistic missile in one of the nine ICBM bases that surrounded Spokane in the first half of the 1960s, Colonel Jeffrey encountered what the Fairchild Air Force Base newspaper described as an "Idaho Welcome" from direct descendents of Spokane Garry. There is no record if the Garrys were aware that Jeffrey had praised Wright and equated his actions in the Indian War with that of the role of the ICBM in the Cold War. (*Fairchild Times*)**

Wright clashed with Spokane, Couer d' Alene, and Palouse Indians in the Battle of Four Lakes on September 1, 1858. The fighting took place approximately twelve miles southwest of the spot where white settlers would one day establish the City of Spokane. Wright and the Indians fought again on September 5, 1858, in the "Battle of Spokane Plains," a dozen miles west of the future site of Spokane. During the two battles, the Indians attempted a defense from Wright's long-range guns and artillery by taking cover in ravines and behind rocks, trees, and bushes, but Wright's weapons were so great that the colonel was able to knock the Indians from their shelters and force them to retreat.[25]

In the course of his campaign, Wright summarily executed sixteen Indians, slaughtered a herd of 800 to 900 Indian horses, destroyed Indian food stores, and uttered a doomsday threat to the Indians that made Khrushchev's cry of "We will bury you!" sound like a greeting from Hallmark. Wright's harrowing remark came on September 7, 1858, when he met with Chief Garry of the Spokane Indians. Lawrence Kip, one of Wright's lieutenants, recorded that Wright told Garry:

> I did not come into this country to ask you to make peace; I came here to fight. Now, when you are tired of war and ask for peace, I will tell you what you must do. You must come to me with your arms, with your women and children, and everything you have, and lay them at my feet. You must put your faith in me and trust to my mercy. If you do this, I shall then tell you the terms upon which I will give you peace. If you do not do this, war will be made upon you this year and the next, and until your nations shall be exterminated.[26]

"Colonel Wright," observed a 1974 Spokane history book edited by Joseph C. Brown, "smote the Indians with the A-bomb of the day." In the book, the "A-bomb" comment meant that Wright's use of long-range guns against the Indians had been devastating, but the tenor of Wright's ultimatum was a close match to the saber-rattling rhetoric that inspired nuclear terror in citizens around the world during the Cold War. However, in Wright's case the war wasn't cold. The fallout from Wright's attack employing long-range weapons, summary executions, and a threat to commit mass murder, terrorized the Indians and dispossessed them of their land. Historian Robert Ignatius Burns, S.J., wrote that the Wright campaign "definitively opened to settlement the vast reaches of Washington Territory." According to historian Clifford E.

Trafzer, "the United States forced many non-reservation Indians onto the reservations and opened their former homes to white settlers." In the 1870s, a group of those settlers established the town of Spokane Falls (amending the name of the town to Spokane in 1891). Spokane's first organized civil defense efforts and the echoes of Wright's threat of exterminating the Indians were a part of the early township.[27]

During the Nez Perce war of 1877, Spokane Falls residents improvised their community's first civil defense shelter when they took refuge in James Glover's general store, which was probably the strongest and safest structure in town. With help from local Indians, Spokane Falls residents also built fortifications on Havermale Island. These measures were meant to protect area residents from a group of Nez Perce Indians who had set up a temporary camp in the area. The white settlers feared that the Nez Perce might be preparing to attack them. According to Glover, the war scare was resolved when he met with local non-Nez Perce Indians and conjured up the memory of Wright's visit to the region:

> My friends, I know where Uncle Sam's soldiers are. They are very near here, and I can call them here at any hour. Do you want to have the last remnants of your people wiped from the face of the earth? If you do not, see that these [Nez Perce] Indians leave here and leave here for good before noon.[28]

Glover's intimidation persuaded the Indians around Spokane to prevail upon the Nez Perce to leave, and Spokane residents did not turn to shelters of a civilian defense type again until WWII.

III. World War II Shelters, 1941–1945

In they came, a baker's dozen of them, boys and girls, trailing to the basement shelter.

—Mrs. Fred B. Huerlin

According to a June 1942 poll, taken during World War II by the American Association of University Women, about half of Spokane's population believed that the Japanese might strike their city. Japanese attacks along the west coast of North America contributed to Spokane's perceived vulnerability. On June 3, 1942, Japanese planes raided Dutch Harbor, Alaska. The next day, they struck again. American casualties from the two assaults amounted to forty-three dead and fifty wounded. The top headline on the front page of the *Spokane Daily Chronicle* screamed in tall upper-case letters: "ALASKA IS BOMBED BY THE JAPANESE." A. T. Amos, Spokane's Civil Defense Council coordinator, framed the Alaska attack as a lesson for Spokane residents. "It is unfortunate that Dutch Harbor was the recipient of a Japanese attack," Amos acknowledged, "but if it helps in making our people realize that this is war—total war—and that we here in Spokane are subject to enemy attack as well as the men in uniform, it will serve a good purpose." Amos' words were underscored eighteen days later when the *Spokane Daily Chronicle* revealed that a Japanese submarine had launched a fifteen minute artillery assault against Fort Stevens near Seaside, Oregon. Fortunately, no one was hurt in the June 22, 1943, attack. Japanese shells hit a small section of road, a tree, and a swampy area.[29]

After the Japanese had attacked Alaska and taken potshots at Oregon, T. C. Edwards, the chairman of the Washington State Defense Council, warned the Spokane region that its "war plants and military installations would be important targets for short raids by enemy planes, with the trip from the Coast an obstacle not too difficult to overcome." Edwards was partly right that the Spokane area was vulnerable to attack from the Japanese but not in the way that he imagined. During WWII, the Japanese attacked the North American continent, including the Spokane area, with a weapon that historian Robert C. Mikesh calls a precursor to the intercontinental ballistic missile: the balloon bomb. On November 3, 1944, the Japanese began releasing balloons from the Japanese mainland that were designed to carry bombs across the Pacific Ocean and strike randomly at targets in the United States. Of 9,000 balloons that the Japanese released, about 1,000 made it to the North American continent. The balloon bombs landed at sites that ranged from California to Michigan and Alaska to Mexico. Not every balloon bomb was accounted for, but they are known to have caused two small fires and taken out a power line that fed the Hanford Atomic Works, which triggered a three-day disruption of plutonium production. At least two bomb-carrying balloons floated over the Spokane region. On February 12, 1945, two unexploded bombs, an incendiary bomb and an anti-personnel bomb, were found by a dump located seven miles north of Spokane. On February 21, 1945, a similar bomb combination was discovered in Spokane. To keep the Japanese in the dark about the partial success of their balloon bomb barrage, the U.S. Office of

Censorship asked the media to keep the balloons a secret from the public. Military authorities revealed the existence of the balloons only in May 1945, after a woman and five children in Oregon discovered an object they could not identify that turned out to be a balloon bomb that exploded and killed the entire group.[30]

Aside from the Japanese balloon bombs, the Spokane area did not suffer a direct attack from the Japanese. To the contrary of the warning from Edwards, the Japanese did not send any planes to conduct air raids against the Spokane region. However, if Japanese planes had flown over the area, Edwards was correct that they would have found targets worth striking. Spokane and Spokane County had industrial works and military sites that lent vital support to the Allied war effort.

During World War II, the Spokane area was home to aluminum plants, the Galena Army Air Depot, Geiger Field, the Velox Navy Depot, and Fort George Wright. The Aluminum Co. of America (ALCOA) processed aluminum at plants in Mead and Trentwood. The Mead facility was an aluminum reduction plant, while the Trentwood operation rolled aluminum into sheets that could be used to manufacture aircraft. Eleven Army Air Corps B-17 bomber groups trained at Geiger Field between 1942 and 1943. The Spokane Army Air Depot (informally designated the Galena Army Air Depot) repaired aircraft engines. Three women triumphantly repaired the 10,000[th] engine serviced at the depot in June 1945. Fort George Wright, an Army post built in 1898 for infantry troops, served as a sub-post of the Spokane Army Air Depot beginning in 1941. The Naval Supply Depot at Velox was commissioned in Spokane in January 1943 and constructed on a square-mile piece of property on the eastern edge of the city. The depot handled, among other things, medical goods, Lend-Lease supplies bound for the Soviet Union, and parts for boats that landed American soldiers on battlefield beaches in the Pacific.[31]

Even before the Spokane region sprouted bases and plants to support America's fight against the Axis, blackouts had become a part of life in the area. The U.S. Army ordered lights out in Spokane the day after the Japanese struck Pearl Harbor. Military officials instructed Spokanites to cover windows and extinguish all outside illumination to frustrate any Japanese pilots who might try to navigate by the city's electric glow.[32]

To black out the windows of a home or a business, a thick curtain would do the trick, but the Crest Line Lumber Co. at North 1601 Division sold a "3-ply veneer" that would darken a window with more precision. Covering windows with tape also kept light from pouring outside, but Joseph K. Carson, an official from the U.S. Office of Civil Defense, frowned on this method. He said that tape should be reserved for medical purposes and declared it was "unpatriotic" to waste it in blacking out windows. The Davenport Hotel would have pleased Carson because it covered its skylight windows with black tar. Workers scraped away the last visible presence of the hotel's World War II air raid precautions during a remodeling project in 1993.[33]

Surprisingly, after military officials ordered the December 8, 1941, blackout of Spokane, they cancelled their order the same day. Many Spokanites missed the counter-order and blacked out their windows. Two days after the half-baked blackout, Major General Millard F. Harmon clarified the Army's position on blackouts in the area. "The location of the Inland Empire," Harmon explained, "is considered to be such that scheduled black-outs during any predictable future will not be necessary."[34]

Spokane chose to go dark voluntarily. The city held three city-wide blackout tests. The rallying cry of Spokane's first blackout exercise on December 7, 1942, was "remember Pearl Harbor and turn your lights out."[35]

"Blackout" means "lights out"—indoors and outside.

Figure 13   **During WWII, The Washington State Defense Council, a twenty-member body which included Governor Arthur B. Langlie and Phil W. Alexander representing Spokane, published** *Civilian Protection* **to instruct people to prepare for possible enemy air raids. (Author's Collection)**

Wayne C. MacGregor was a teenager living in Spokane when the blackout tests began. He recalled in his World War II memoir, *Through These Portals*: "Rather than causing apprehension among my friends and I, the blackouts were an excuse for turning out the lights and trying to make time with a girlfriend while on a date." There were other maneuvers in the dark. During a blackout exercise on March 25, 1943, Mrs. Herbert Pitz gave birth to a baby boy at Deaconess Hospital. In the same blackout, police arrested John O'Brien for refusing to turn off the lights of his home at West 1925 Twenty-Fifth Street. Unfortunately for Julian Thorsness, police were not on hand in the darkness of a blacked-out pub when someone threatened him with a sharp object and stole his wallet. The final blackout exercise in Spokane took place October 1, 1943. During the test, city officials directed drivers to pull off the roads, shut down their car engines, and turn off their headlights. William Groce, the director of civilian protection of the Washington State Defense Council, observed the blackout test, and he marveled to see "Riverside so clear of traffic that you could have fired a cannon down it without hitting anyone."[36]

Blacking out windows and turning out lights were not the only steps taken to fortify Spokane. The city also turned to shelters. While Spokane officials had been enthusiastic about blackouts from the beginning of World War II, they were slower to endorse shelters. In January 1942, a *Spokane Daily Chronicle* reader wrote to the paper and asked for advice to help set up a "safety cellar." The paper forwarded the reader's request for guidance to Perry E. Dye, the city's executive secretary of civil defense. Dye said, "Forget it." He was skeptical about home shelters because "to be really efficient an air raid shelter would have to be gas-proofed and air conditioned, an extremely costly undertaking." Furthermore, Dye argued, "In the event of an air raid, the housewife will be safe in her own kitchen, providing she remains away from windows and other spots where she might be injured by fragments, or flying debris. A spot under the table would be just about as safe in most cases as an expensive air raid shelter."[37]

Spokanites turned to shelters of their own accord. On January 14, 1942, the *Spokane Daily Chronicle* reported that business owners in Spokane's downtown area had voluntarily established refuge rooms in their basements and vaults. "Basements," the paper learned from a survey of building managers, "are the most commonly selected refuge because lights can be left on there in a blackout." People set up refuge rooms in their homes as well. On January 14, 1942, the *Spokane Daily Chronicle* featured a picture of Mr. and Mrs. L. J. Matthews standing outside their house in front of a sandbagged window that had once illuminated their basement. The Matthews had designated the basement of their home at South 1124 Cedar as a "black-out" room. It contained sand, buckets, and a fire hose attached to a faucet, all of which would prove helpful if the Matthews had to fight fires caused by enemy bombs or incendiary devices. The *Spokane Daily Chronicle* hailed the Matthews for having one of the "first Spokane homes to become practically 100 per cent [*sic*] equipped for Defense [*sic*] against air raids and chemical warfare."[38]

It is unclear how many Spokane businesses and homeowners bucked Dye's dismissal of shelters and followed the Matthews' example. Newspaper records show that at least one prominent Spokane family embraced shelters: the Cowles. In the early months of America's entry into the war, the Citizens Realty Company—owned by the Cowles family—proposed a public air raid shelter in Spokane and coverage of the idea appeared in the *Spokesman-Review*—another enterprise owned by the Cowles family. The Citizens Realty Company made their advocacy of shelters known after the War Department confiscated a load of steel that the company had planned to use to build a parking garage at Main and Post. The company offered that the unfinished garage could be a public air raid shelter if the government could be convinced to release enough steel to finish its construction. They succeeded in winning an endorsement of their shelter idea from Spokane's City Council and the Spokane Civil Defense Council. The War Production Board conceded that the unfinished construction was blocking part of the street and impeding traffic, and gave the company permission to have supplies to complete the parking garage to street level. An article in the *Spokane Daily Chronicle*—another large newspaper in Spokane owned by the Cowles family—proclaimed jubilantly, "A huge downtown air-raid shelter soon may be ready for Spokane folk!"[39]

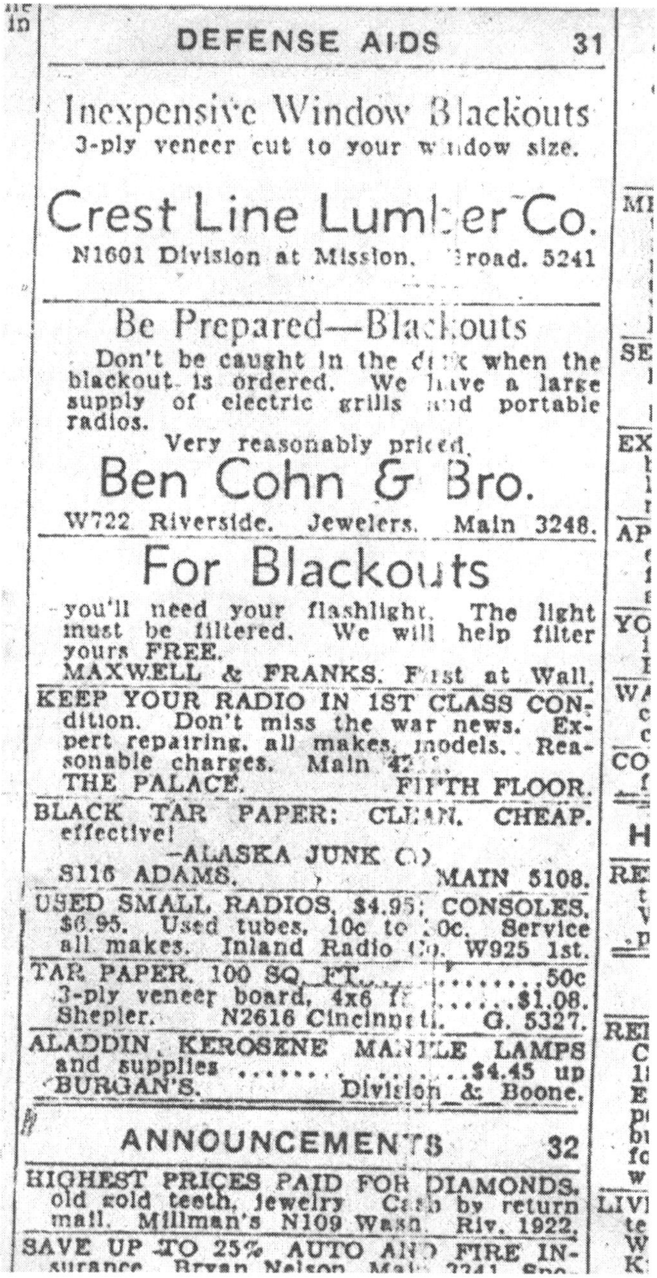

DEFENSE AIDS   31

Inexpensive Window Blackouts
3-ply veneer cut to your window size.

Crest Line Lumber Co.
N1601 Division at Mission. Broad. 5241

Be Prepared—Blackouts
Don't be caught in the dark when the blackout is ordered. We have a large supply of electric grills and portable radios.
Very reasonably priced.

Ben Cohn & Bro.
W722 Riverside. Jewelers. Main 3248.

For Blackouts
you'll need your flashlight. The light must be filtered. We will help filter yours FREE.
MAXWELL & FRANKS. First at Wall.

KEEP YOUR RADIO IN 1ST CLASS CONdition. Don't miss the war news. Expert repairing. all makes. models. Reasonable charges. Main 47.
THE PALACE.   FIFTH FLOOR.

BLACK TAR PAPER: CLEAN. CHEAP. effective!
—ALASKA JUNK CO.
S116 ADAMS.   MAIN 5108.

USED SMALL RADIOS, $4.95; CONSOLES, $6.95. Used tubes. 10c to 30c. Service all makes. Inland Radio Co. W925 1st.

TAR PAPER. 100 SQ. FT. 50c
3-ply veneer board, 4x6 ft. . . . . . $1.08.
Shepler.   N2616 Cincinnati.   G. 5327.

ALADDIN KEROSENE MANTLE LAMPS
and supplies . . . . $4.45 up
BURGAN'S.   Division & Boone.

ANNOUNCEMENTS   32

HIGHEST PRICES PAID FOR DIAMONDS. old gold teeth. jewelry Cash by return mail. Millman's N109 Wash. Riv. 1922.

SAVE UP TO 25% AUTO AND FIRE INsurance Bryan Nelson Mai. 3241 Spo.

Figure 14   "Defense Aids," a classified ad section in the January 30, 1942, *Spokane Daily Chronicle*, sold blackout materials and civil defense goods.

Perhaps due in part to the lobbying of the Citizens Realty Company, Spokane city officials approved a public shelter system and established twenty public air raid shelters in time to include them in the city's first official blackout exercise, held one year after the Japanese attack on Pearl Harbor. The shelter accommodations ranged from the posh Davenport Hotel to the Howard Street lavatory under the Northern Pacific viaduct. Spokane's chief building inspector, Arthur G. Hoefer, chose the shelter sites in buildings made of concrete and steel. "Though they will not afford protection from a direct hit by a bomb," Hoefer explained, "they are adequate to protect the public from fragments and from explosions in the street." Seven of the buildings Hoefer chose to serve as shelters—the State Theater, the Crescent Store, the Elks Temple, the Symons Building, the Paulsen Building, City Ramp garage, and the Davenport Hotel—would re-enlist as fallout shelters during the Cold War. Hoefer's other shelters included a Payless Drugstore "now nearing completion" at Main and Post, the Garden Bowling Alley and Garage, the Realty Building, the Fox Theater, the Liberty Theater, Western Union, the Jensen-Byrd parking lot, the Rookery Building, the Spokane and Eastern Building, the Washington Trust Building, the Medical and Dental Building Garage, and the Welch Building. In addition to the city shelters designated by Hoefer, the Red Cross set up five shelters of its own. During the December 7, 1942, blackout drill, it operated air raid shelter emergency centers at Lewis and Clark High School, Rogers High School, Libby Junior High School, Havermale Junior High School, and Logan Grade School. Two of these schools, Libby Junior High and Havermale Junior High, would host fallout shelters during the Cold War.[40]

Figure 15   Arthur G. Hoefer, Spokane's building inspector and architect of Spokane's public shelter program during WWII, points to a basement hideaway in a drawing displaying "relative danger during an air raid." The picture also shows two kinds of backyard bunkers, buried and partially-buried. Hoefer's assistant here is Spokane City Chemist Roger G. James. According to a note in a Spokane civil defense scrapbook from WWII, this photo appeared in the *Spokane Daily Chronicle* on April 18, 1942. However, this citation is not certain since the photo does not appear in Washington State University's microfilm copies of the *Spokane Daily Chronicle* or its rival paper, the *Spokesman-Review*, for that day or month. (Washington State Archives, Eastern Region Branch, Cheney. Hereafter referred to as WSA, ERB, Cheney.)

"When the alarm comes, go to the refuge room"

Figure 16 "Refuge room," "blackout room," and "air raid shelter" became a part of Spokane's vocabulary during World War II. The Washington State Defense Council's handbook, *Civilian Protection,* instructed residents to flee to these shelters at the sound of air raid warnings. (Author's Collection)

Some of Spokane's shelters were reserved for children only. Three hundred women of the Spokane Council of Parents and Teachers block mother program volunteered to turn their homes into refuges for any children who were caught between home and school during an air raid. Mrs. Fred B. Huerlin, one of the block mothers, helped publicize the shelter program by hosting a children's gathering in the basement of her home at West 3803 Longfellow. In the October 12, 1942, issue of the *Spokane Daily Chronicle*, she described the children's arrival: "In they came, a baker's dozen of them, boys and girls, trailing to the basement shelter." The children played with toys and a cat named "Blitz." After Mrs. Huerlin served the kids hot cocoa and cookies, a boy asked, "When can we come again?" Mrs. Huerlin answered: "Most any time." To *Spokane Daily Chronicle* readers she confided, "It was just too bad to tell him to 'wait until there is an air raid.'"[41]

As the war turned in favor of the Allies, Spokanites judged that blackouts and air raid shelters were increasingly unnecessary. Spokanite Arthur J. Freeborg probably summarized a popular sentiment when he wrote in a March 1943 letter-to-the-editor, "I feel certain that we could discard almost all phases of Civilian Defense without jeopardizing the safety of our land or people." Perry Dye, the executive secretary of the Spokane Civilian Defense Council, confirmed to reporters in April 1943 that the public was losing interest in civil defense. In May 1943, the *Spokane Daily Chronicle* described the public's interest in civil defense as "lagging." On November 16, 1943, the *Spokane Daily Chronicle* reported that the City of Spokane had decided to stop holding blackout drills.[42]

In the late afternoon of August 14, 1945, Spokane City Hall triggered the city's air raid sirens to announce the surrender of Japan. The sirens, which the city had depended on to warn citizens of enemy attack and instigate blackouts, failed to sound. Firemen determined that the relay batteries had "burned out." Picking up the slack, the city's fire department sirens, newsboys, horn-tooting motorists, and jubilant crowds spread the word that World War II was over.[43]

The Japanese surrender followed the U.S. atomic bombing of Hiroshima on August 6, 1945, and Nagasaki on August 9. Two days after Hiroshima had been destroyed, the Associated Press issued a story that sixty percent of the city had been leveled by the bomb and the firestorm it had created. The AP painted a grisly picture of the destruction: "In the heart of the city only a few concrete structures remain standing. They were believed to be air raid shelters. Even they had been burned inside." In contemplation of the atomic bomb's devastating power, the *Spokesman-Review* editorialized under the headline, "Terrifying Force Loose in World," that "science may have provided mankind with a means of destroying himself and all his works." That possibility seemed likelier after the Soviet Union tested its first atomic bomb on August 29, 1949. When the U.S. embarked on the Korean War in June and July 1950, fighting communists allied with the Soviet Union, people in the Spokane region worried that the Korean conflict might be a preamble to nuclear war, and began to make plans for civil defense against the "terrifying force."[44]

IV. Early Cold War Civil Defense Schemes, 1951–1958

All you kids must be ready for a new danger—the Atomic Bomb.

—Bert the Turtle

Less than a year before Superintendent John A. Shaw would bow to pressure from Spokane attorney and civil rights crusader Carl Maxey and shake up the racially homogenous ranks of Spokane's all-white teacher corps by hiring a black teacher, Shaw called a meeting of every public school principal and teacher in Spokane on December 7, 1950—the ninth anniversary of the Japanese attack on Pearl Harbor. Shaw warned the crowd of over 900 educators assembled at Spokane's Lewis and Clark High School auditorium that "the same thing that happened to Hiroshima and Nagasaki could happen here, and we must prepare for it." Shaw's speech, or news of it, may have been persuasive to Spokane Civil Defense Coordinator Leighton L. Dugger. Two days after Shaw's remarks, Dugger announced a Spokane building survey to find suitable sites for bomb shelters. The result of the survey evidently was not encouraging. Dugger later told the press that Spokane's existing buildings would not make suitable homes for air raid shelters. He also said that the cost of building new shelters for the public was "absolutely prohibitive."[45]

Cost was a sure-fire sticking point in civil defense planning. In 1951, the Federal Civil Defense Administration (F.C.D.A.) hoped to use taxpayer money to construct blast shelters that would offer U.S. citizens comprehensive protection from nuclear attack, but Congress said no. President Eisenhower said no, too, when the F.C.D.A. pitched a $13 billion public fallout shelter program in August 1956. In response to the government's refusal to fund expensive shelter projects, federal civil defense leaders began promoting thrifty measures to guard against atomic attack.[46]

Some of the most fiscally austere methods to protect the public had been outlined in a U.S. National Security Resources Board (N.S.R.B.) publication called *Survival Under Atomic Attack*. The booklet gave the public "six survival secrets." The first secret was that if you were under attack, you should "get down in a basement or subway. Should you unexpectedly be caught out-of-doors, seek shelter alongside a building, or jump in any handy ditch or gutter." In 1951, the N.S.R.B. distributed 20 million copies of *Survival Under Atomic Attack*, and its influence seems to have extended to Spokane. In an apparent adaptation of the pamphlet's economical suggestion to "jump in any handy ditch or gutter," Col. C. S. Phelps of Spokane's Civilian Defense Advisory Council told Spokanites on March 2, 1951, that in the event of a nuclear attack they could take shelter along the city's riverbanks, which was to essentially say, go jump in the river.[47]

Another civil defense scheme that had an obvious economy was advocated by Bert the Turtle, a childrens' cartoon spokesperson for the Federal Civil Defense Administration. In an animated film, a comic strip, and a sound recording, Bert told children to "duck and cover" if they detected the bright flash of an atom bomb explosion. In the first Bert the Turtle comic strip that appeared in the *Spokane Daily Chronicle* April 21, 1952, Bert was menaced by a monkey with a firecracker, an analogy to the threat of an atomic-armed Soviet Union. To escape the monkey's firecracker blast, Bert ducked his head into the cover of his shell. The comic narration explained that Bert "has his shelter on his back" and advised readers, "you must learn to find shelter." In tune with Bert the Turtle's mantra of "duck and cover," Spokane area teachers instructed school children to hide under their desks during civil defense drills. Bert's message spread beyond the classroom when Spokane County Civil Defense Coordinator C. J. Chaffins approved of Bert's tactics and recommended the comic to adults. "By giving a little thought to the ideas presented by 'Bert the Turtle'," Chaffins claimed, "a person can pretty well figure out for himself and his family what to do in case of a bomb attack."[48]

In 1953, Spokane Civil Defense Coordinator Leighton L. Dugger announced a plan to supplement "duck and cover" with "walk and cover" when he asked for people caught in downtown Spokane during an atomic attack to walk out of the area and "seek survival behind rocks and other rough ground." Eight days after Dugger asked that Spokanites hide behind rocks, he reversed his position on the inadvisability of establishing shelters. The *Spokane Daily Chronicle* reported on March 28, 1953, that Dugger was preparing to send letters to twenty-five building owners proposing that they allow their structures to be used as air raid shelters. According to the newspaper, Dugger suggested that in the event of an attack, the shelters should be available only for businesses in the buildings and their customers. Dugger's plan, the *Spokane Daily Chronicle* wrote, "suggests that the general public be kept out of the buildings, except the aged, infirm and mothers with children." The details of Dugger's customers-only shelters, whether, for instance, the Spokane businesses that had a record of refusing to serve black people would be allowed to deny black people access to shelters (except for the aged, infirm and mothers with children), were never made clear because Dugger's plan was torn to shreds.[49]

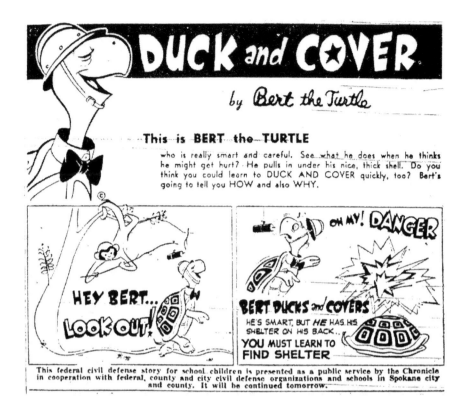

Figure 17 Bert the Turtle dodged a monkey with a firecracker in a cartoon that appeared in the *Spokane Daily Chronicle* on April 21, 1952. In another Bert episode that appeared in the paper that month, he advised children: "Your teachers, your parents and the Civil Defense workers in your city know how dangerous atomic bombs are. If there is time you will hear a special warning signal, probably a siren or a whistle or a horn. Then you must go at once to a shelter. Grownups will tell you where to go and they will help you get there." The *Chronicle* printed the comics because Spokane and Spokane County civil defense organizations had no funds to buy the Bert comics for Spokane area school children. (*Spokane Daily Chronicle*)

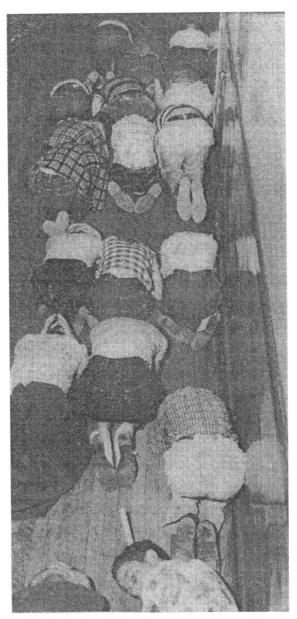

Figure 18   Just as Bert the Turtle had advised, students
from Spokane's Finch School "duck and cover."
They acted in concert with 25,000 other Spokane
school children as part of a "yellow alert" civil
defense drill held May 26, 1954. (*Spokane Daily
Chronicle*)

A year after Dugger prepared his shelter planning letters to building owners, federal and state officials threw out the notion of establishing shelters. They advocated a new strategy: evacuating cities to protect urban populations from nuclear attack.[50]

Federal Civil Defense head Val Peterson lectured the nation in the pages of the April 5, 1954, edition of *Newsweek*, "We think that if a hydrogen bomb is exploded over your city, there is only one way you can be certain of saving your life, and that is not to be in the city." Consequently, Peterson demanded, "We must have tests in which entire cities are evacuated." Washington State Civil Defense Director D. E. Barbey was in step with the national civil defense leader's thinking. On April 26, 1954, Barbey declared, "The old theory of bomb shelters is now obsolete. We must find ways to disperse." Spokane civil defense leaders obliged the higher-ups in the civil defense hierarchy by creating an evacuation plan. The Spokane strategy called for residents, upon receipt of advance warning of an impending nuclear attack, to flee the downtown area on foot. Outside the core of the city, evacuees were supposed to meet buses that would ferry them to safe zones where civil defense planners figured that the "brows of hills" would shelter people from danger.[51]

To test how quickly Spokanites could head for the hills, John J. Lenhart, Dugger's successor as city civil defense director, in collaboration with Washington State civil defense officials, the Army National Guard, and the Air Force, launched a massive evacuation exercise called "Operation Walkout" on a rainy day on April 26, 1954. Spokane civil defense officials signaled the cry of the city's air raid sirens at 9:35 AM, and prodded thousands of Spokanites to flee from downtown.

Spokane residents had been briefed on the exercise by civil defense leaders and local newspapers. In addition, one-hundred-fifty Boy Scouts and junior police covered Spokane on Friday,

April 23, 1954, distributing leaflets that read, "The eyes of the nation will be on Spokane. . . cooperate for Spokane because this may save your life some day." According to varied estimates from Washington State and Spokane area civil defense officials, local and national reporters, and observers from the National Research Council, 10,000 to 19,000 Spokanites participated in the exercise.[52]

During Operation Walkout, as thousands of people fled Spokane, the 161st National Guard Infantry Regiment commanded by Col. Ralph T. Phelps, took up positions on Spokane's street corners to maintain order. One hundred guardsmen bearing rifles affixed with bayonets patrolled downtown. Two tanks from the regiment guarded Riverside. Members of the 161st held 30-caliber machine gun positions on four Spokane rooftops, and they fired blanks at three Air Force F-86D Sabre jets that buzzed the city to imitate a battle taking place. The Sabre jets were part of the 445th F-I Squadron based at Geiger Field, and they were flown by 2d Lt. E. F. Bures, 2d Lt. D. H. Zimmerman, and 1st Lt. R. C. Shannon. The *Spokane Daily Chronicle* reported that "one fighter did a roll directly over the city." The director of the Washington State Civil Defense Administration, Daniel E. Barbey, confided to Federal Civil Defense Administration head Val Peterson that the Sabre jets "appeared narrowly to miss colliding with a Civil Air Patrol plane flying at low level to observe the operations."

Before the exercise, Spokane firemen had planned to set off explosions at their fire stations at the appearance of Air Force bombers to simulate bomb bursts, but on the day of the exercise, the firemen jumped their cue and triggered the explosions before the planes arrived over the city. Despite the lack of appropriately timed sound effects, B-25, B-36, and B-29 bombers made impressive sweeps over the city.[53]

Figure 19 Researchers asked walkers what they would do in a real attack. They answered: "I would high-tail it home, grab my family and get out quick."; "Run like hell."; and "I really don't know." This photo of the April 26, 1954, exercise appeared in *Parade* magazine and was reprinted in *Spokane: Your Civil Defense Manual*, 1956. (Author's Collection)

"WALKOUT" leaflets fell on Northwest side.

FAIRCHILD B-36 flew over city during test.

Figure 20   A B-29 bomber struck a morbid punctuation to the theatrics of Operation Walkout, dropping leaflets illustrated with the black silhouette of a bomb and a bold warning in capital letters: "THIS COULD HAVE BEEN AN 'H' BOMB." The images above appeared in the *Spokesman Review* and were collected in a Spokane Civil Defense Scrapbook. (WSA, ERB, Cheney)

In a mat
after John
defense dir
yellow ale
school ad
more than
installation

Figure 21   Leaflets decorated with a graphic of an "H" bomb littered the area northwest of downtown Spokane after they fell from a B-36 that made a mock air raid on the city. Researchers from the National Research Council noted, in criticism of the practical applications of Operation Walkout, that the leaflets landed "near one of the theoretical evacuation zones." A Spokane civil defense scrapbook ascribes this photograph to the *Spokesman-Review*. (WSA, ERB, Cheney)

In numbers of public participants, Operation Walkout was a success—but civil defense authorities eventually realized that the evacuation strategy was flawed because missiles could fall out of the sky without giving the public any warning time to evacuate and even if people did manage to flee the city before it was struck, they would be vulnerable to radioactive fallout. Spokane area resident Mrs. C. M. Lockwood attended a civil defense conference in Washington, D.C. in 1958, and she announced a change in civil defense strategy when she returned home. She said that shelters were now necessary because "evacuation techniques—moving a city's entire population from a targeted area—has been made impractical." Steuart Pittman, Director of the Federal Office of Civil Defense, an organization that succeeded the F.D.C.A. and operated under the auspices of the Department of Defense, officially acknowledged that "evacuation of urban areas before attack is no longer feasible as national policy" in November 1961. Pittman made this announcement in a letter to Wisconsin Congressional Representative Robert W. Kastenmeir. In his letter, Pittman clarified his position by adding, "In certain localities uniquely situated evacuation may still be feasible, but in general we know that a short warning time in the missile age and the long reach of fallout require reorientation of many local plans around the movement of people into nearby shelters." Spokane County Civil Defense Director Clyde J. Chaffins, who had endorsed evacuation over shelters in 1955 because he thought "it would be folly to go underground to escape an atom blast," rethought that position and aligned himself with Pittman as a critic of evacuation. Chaffins said,

> If an enemy bomb or rocket missed its target, assuming the city or places near the city were the target, or if more than one bomb were dropped, persons trying to evacuate the city might travel directly into the path of the missile. They might also put themselves into a dangerous fallout area— even more dangerous than in the city.

By 1961, Chaffins was advising Spokane residents, "Build the best shelter you can afford."[54]

V. Backyard Bunkers and Basement Hideaways, 1953–1962

We should do everything we can to get people interested in building shelters.

—City of Spokane Councilman Gus H. Nieman

In December 1958, Spokane was confronted by thirty billboards that showed a painting of an atomic mushroom cloud looming prominently over the order, "protect yourself from fallout." The billboards advertised a federal booklet entitled *Facts about Fallout Protection*. To survive fallout, the booklet advised, "the best protection is an underground shelter with at least three feet of earth or sand above it. Two feet of concrete will give the same protection. If the shelter has an adequate door and air filter, it will give you almost complete protection." For serviceable protection of the less-than-ideal but better-than-nothing variety, it recommended a "basement refuge" of sandbags piled around a wooden frame to block out radiation. "If you want to build a basement shelter with concrete or sandbagged walls and ceiling," the booklet continued, "plans are available," and it urged, "consult your local civil defense officials." Two years later, Spokane Civil Defense Director Clyde H. Friend, reinforced the message to reporters, "We are encouraging the construction of home bomb shelters."

Figure 22   Advertising saves. A person could read the federal government's message to "protect yourself from fallout" on thirty Spokane area billboards in 1958. (WSA, SGA, Olympia)

Newspaper stories from the Spokane area indicated that a handful of homeowners in the Spokane region had responded to advice from civil defense authorities and built backyard bunkers and basement hideaways in the years immediately after the mushroom cloud billboard appeared, but an upswell of public enthusiasm for fallout shelters did not occur until President Kennedy's Berlin Crisis speech in the summer of 1961. After President Kennedy's talk, Spokane city civil defense officials reported they were getting lots of calls from residents seeking advice about fallout shelters. The officials also described an increased amount of shelter building.[55]

Kennedy had vaguely endorsed building family fallout shelters in his Berlin Crisis broadcast—historian Walter Karp wrote that Kennedy had "obliquely suggested" it—but the public responded to Kennedy's speech as if he had asked them to start digging bunkers in their backyards and begin shoring up their basements immediately.[56]

Figure 23   "The best protection," the 1958 Federal Civil Defense Administration booklet advised, "is an underground shelter with at least three feet of earth or sand above it. Two feet of concrete will give the same protection. If the shelter has an adequate door and an air filter, it will give you almost complete protection." (Author's collection)

The confrontational course of the Berlin Crisis added to the public's motivation to find refuge from atomic attack. In August 1961, communists sealed the border between East and West Berlin and laid barbed-wire tracings that became the foundation for the Berlin Wall. Amidst the escalating Cold War tension, Spokane Civil Defense Director Clyde H. Friend reported on September 1, 1961, that private shelter contractors were catching plenty of work. That same day, the Soviet Union threw out their own moratorium on nuclear weapons testing and began a series of nuclear test blasts that meant more boom times for shelter builders. The climax of the nuclear tests occurred two months later when Khrushchev's scientists set off their record-shattering thermonuclear super bomb.[57]

While the Soviet weapons testing series was gearing up to set records for destructive power and the Berlin Crisis was simmering, President Kennedy endorsed a section of a September 15, 1961, issue of *Life* magazine that featured blueprints and drawings to help readers engineer "A Simple Room in Basement Built with Concrete Blocks," "Big Pipe in the Backyard under Three Feet of Earth," "A Double-walled Bunker for Safety above Ground," and other projects that would offer shelter against fallout. Perhaps in response to this development, the Spokane city government decided, in the words of Councilman Gus H. Nieman, "We should do everything we can to get people interested in building shelters." In a council meeting held eleven days after the appearance of the issue of *Life* magazine devoted to shelters, Mayor Neal R. Fosseen proposed that building permit fees be waived for people constructing fallout shelters. Councilman Del E. Jones and Councilman J. C. Kopet agreed. Kopet said, "We should make every concession in order to get them built."[58]

On September 27, 1961, Spokane's City Manager Henry B. Nabers asked lawyers to draft an ordinance that would make it possible for residents of Spokane to build fallout shelters without paying building permit fees. Spokane's City Council passed the ordinance on October 16, 1961. That month, Spokane's Building Permit Office issued twenty-six fallout shelter permits. The permits were for backyard bunkers and basement hideaways. Spokane County issued shelter permits, too. On October 13, 1961, the *Spokane Daily Chronicle* reported that C. F. Thackwell, Spokane County's chief building inspector, had given out approximately a dozen shelter permits in the four weeks leading up to October 13.[59]

The public's interest in shelter construction increased, but the permit figures did not take into account the total number of shelters built by Spokanites because homeowners tended to keep their shelters secret. Sam C. Guess, chairman of the Spokane Municipal League's Subcommittee on Individual and Family Shelters, reported near the end of November 1961, "We are informed that many people have erected shelters without permits merely because they didn't want it known that they had shelters." According to a 1962 *Spokesman-Review* article by Joel Ream, "Most people, of course, 'bootlegged' in a few bricks at a time and worked as quietly as possible. Only so much food and air would be available in the shelters and although everyone loves his neighbor, it was going to be every man for himself in the emergency."[60]

The secrecy surrounding shelter construction makes it impossible to obtain an exact count of shelters built in the United States, Washington State, and Spokane. However, rough guesses are available. Congress estimated that there were at least 1,565 home fallout shelters in the United States in 1960. With the caveat that "all home shelters have not been reported to this office," Washington State Civil Defense Director Charles C. Ralls informed Congressman Chet Holifield on February 24, 1960, that Washington State had approximately 200 home shelters. Burt

Jesmore, a contractor in the shelter building business, told a Spokane newspaper in August 1960 that he guessed there were twenty-five family shelters in Spokane. The presumed number of private shelters in Spokane grew throughout the 1960s. On January 2, 1967, the *Spokane Daily Chronicle* reported that an official of the City of Spokane's Civil Defense Department—the name of the official was not revealed—estimated that Spokane had three-hundred private fallout shelters. Near the end of the decade, Spokane Civil Defense Director Clyde H. Friend probably put it most accurately when he said on November 6, 1969, "There are more private shelters than we know about." Among the shelter owners of Spokane, though, there were at least half-a-dozen survivor-types who were not shy about telling the world they had prepared to weather nuclear war.[61]

Private Bomb and Fallout Shelters, 1953–1961

The plaintiff, gravely concerned for the survival and welfare of his family in the event of a nuclear or thermonuclear war, had constructed, equipped and provisioned a concrete bomb and fall-out shelter on the premises of his home.

—William P. Wimberley

The first news of a private atomic bomb shelter established in the Spokane region broke shortly after Spokane County Civil Defense Director Clyde J. Chaffins personally witnessed an atomic test blast in the Nevada desert on March 17, 1953. The Atomic Energy Commission and the Federal Civil Defense Agency created a sixteen kiloton nuclear explosion to gauge what would happen to full-scale mock ups of residential structures built near the testing site's designated ground zero. Chaffins saw that mannequins in the upstairs of the houses were destroyed in the explosion but dummies in shelters in the basements survived intact. The fact that the mannequins placed underground were not blown to splinters convinced Chaffins to announce to the Spokane public on March 23, 1953, that "simple basement shelters . . . give pretty good protection for people against the effects of the bomb."[62]

On March 27, 1953, four days after Chaffins had given shelters his endorsement, Mr. and Mrs. G. R. Johnson nominated the basement of their home at North 3408 Crestline for duty as a shelter. Charitably, the Johnsons invited forty-seven of their neighbors to join them in their basement if Spokane were to be bombed. The Johnsons' initiative and civic-mindedness entitles them to receive credit for establishing the first private and quasi-public atomic bomb shelter in Spokane.[63]

Approximately one year after the Johnsons had converted their basement into a shelter, civil defense officials adopted evacuation as their preferred strategy for surviving nuclear war, and shelter activity in Spokane became either non-existent or went unreported until late 1958, when the *Spokane Daily Chronicle* announced that Chester L. Brown had built "Spokane's first private bomb shelter." Brown, Spokane's chief radio engineer and chief of Spokane's civil defense communications division, constructed the shelter as a separate underground addition to his home at East 2213 Twenty-ninth.

The *Chronicle* succinctly summed up the details of Brown's refuge:

> 12 feet square, of concrete block construction. The roof is two-foot thick reinforced concrete. There is a two-foot-wide entrance hall from the house with doors at each end and the room has a filtered air intake exhaust pipe and air exhaust with a blower that can be operated by hand in case of a power failure.[64]

Figure 24 (Top) Children first. Chester L. Brown sends his daughters down into their family fallout shelter. (Bottom) Underground, Bonita and Michele Brown are all smiles. Their father thought to provide the family shelter with an elaborate communications system. The photos appeared in a newspaper spread titled "Shelter Is Safe, Homey." A clipping of the spread is in a Spokane Civil Defense Scrapbook. There is no paper name listed with the article, but it is dated March 1960. (WSA, ERB, Cheney)

Spokane's papers did not record the order of construction for the rest of the city's private shelters. However, Wesley S. Wagoner's shelter, mentioned in a short blurb by the *Spokane Daily Chronicle* on September 9, 1960, attracted some of the earliest attention. Little would be known about Wagoner's shelter if its destruction had not become the subject of a lawsuit. Court records and press accounts of the trial created a glimpse of the shelter and the man who built it.[65]

Wagoner's attorney, William P. Wimberley, explained to the Spokane Superior Court that Wagoner had built his "bomb and fall-out shelter" because he was "gravely concerned for the survival and welfare of his family in the event of a nuclear or thermonuclear war." Understandably, Wagoner was upset when a driver from the Audubon Fuel Company entered the backyard of Wagoner's Spokane home at East 1128 Longfellow in mid-December 1960 and fed 599 gallons of oil into the air intake for Wagoner's underground shelter. The oil that funneled into the 10' X 14' bunker made a puddle eleven inches deep.

Audubon accepted responsibility for the oil spill, but it alleged that Wagoner was partly to blame for the mishap because the shelter "vent pipes . . . looked deceptively like oil intake pipes." Wagoner had neglected to warn the company about their similarity. Despite the pipe similarity, Wagoner sought full compensation from the company to restore his shelter to its former condition.

Attorney Wimberley told the court that the shelter was "ruined." He explained that "the earth surrounding the said shelter has been saturated with fuel oil, which emits foul and intolerable odors." According to Wagoner, the only remedy was to remove the shelter and the dirt around it and rebuild the shelter with new materials. To remake the shelter, Wagoner asked the jury to award him $1,750 to excavate his old shelter, $5,000 to build a new shelter, and $2,850 to recover money he had already spent on cleaning and repair. The jury, possibly sympathetic to the fuel company's argument about the look-alike pipes, awarded Wagoner only $3,500.[66]

Wagoner's case did not win him all of the money he had sought, but it succeeded in documenting his status as a pioneer of the home shelter movement in Spokane. Dewey Allsop was another trailblazer. If the oil-flooded Wagoner shelter was the most unfortunate among the earliest known atomic hiding places in Spokane, the Allsop den at North 105 Gillis in Spokane Valley was distinguished, according to the *Spokane Daily Chronicle*, as "one of the most elaborate fallout shelters."[67]

In August 1961, Allsop said he believed that nuclear war was likely and he advised Spokane residents to build a shelter. "Now is the time to build it," he said, "even though we will probably not get hit until 1963." The backyard bunker that Allsop built for his family first came to public attention on March 5, 1961, through the reporting of Kathleen O'Sullivan of the *Spokesman-Review*. Home shelters were evidently enough of a novelty that O'Sullivan felt compelled to attest to the family's sanity. She specified that "the Allsops aren't oddballs." According to O'Sullivan's report, the Allsops—father Dewey, mother Lottie, and daughter Teddy Jane—had a sensible set-up to protect themselves from nuclear war.

Their concrete shelter measured 14 feet by 15 feet and had a domed ceiling with a 7-foot peak. The top of the shelter roof was buried three feet underground. Aside from having the hole in the backyard dug, Allsop, a machinist, did all of the work on the shelter without any help from contractors. By minimizing labor costs, Allsop was able to keep the expense of the shelter to about $750. Spokane County Civil Defense Director Clyde J. Chaffins estimated that the shelter would have cost approximately $1,800 without any added profit if it had been built by a construction company.

To gain quick and discreet access to the shelter, Allsop constructed a tunnel that led from the basement of his family's home to the shelter. He protected the basement entrance to the shelter with a six-inch-thick concrete door. To get out of the shelter in the event something blocked the basement corridor, he built an escape hatch that led from the ceiling of the shelter up to the ground level of the backyard. For camouflage, he hid the concrete door of the escape hatch underneath a birdbath. By August 30, 1961, Allsop was using the birdbath to disguise a periscope. The spy glass, Allsop claimed, would help alleviate "that 'cooped up' feeling which can lead to all kinds of nervous reactions."

The inside of the Allsop shelter was outfitted with other clever touches. The Allsops connected a bicycle to an electric generator to provide themselves with pedal-powered emergency lighting. For warmth, the Allsops planned to rely on their own body heat. While family shelters were typically outfitted with mechanical air blowers operated by hand cranks to refresh the air in the shelters, Allsop created a draft system that automatically exchanged the air in the shelter for outside air without the need for any mechanical aid. Spokane County Civil Defense Director Clyde J. Chaffins was so impressed with Allsop's innovative air filter design that did away with the need for cranking and could, in Chaffins' words, "blow out a lighted match held 6 inches from the outlet without the use of fan or blower," that he sent a description of Allsop's shelter to Washington State Civil Defense Director Charles C. Ralls.[68]

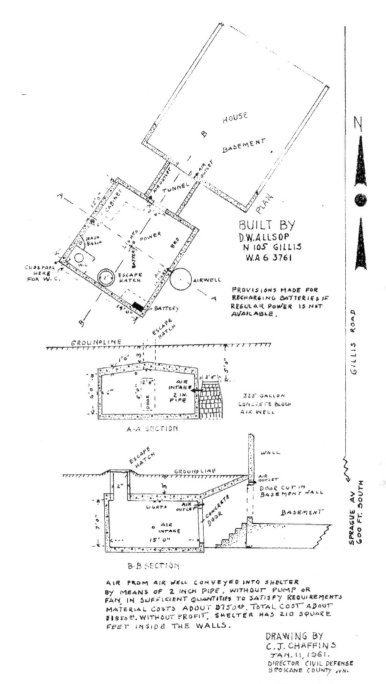

Figure 25   Allsop's shelter. (WSA, SGA, Olympia)

Ideas for shelter construction flowed both ways. To promote federally approved family fallout shelter designs, the federal Office of Civilian and Defense Mobilization financed the construction of demonstration underground fallout shelters for homeowners across the United States. City of Spokane Civil Defense Auxiliary Police Chief Curtis C. Vandervert enrolled in this program, and the government paid for the construction of a fallout shelter in his front yard at North 4227 Cedar.[69]

In March 1960, the Office of Civilian and Defense Mobilization approved a $1,986 bid by a Spokane firm called Northwest Contract to tear up Vandervert's yard and build a six-person demonstration fallout shelter made of steel-reinforced concrete. The shelter was designed to be nine feet, four inches wide, twelve feet long, and six and a half feet tall. The roof of the shelter was intended to sit under two feet of earth.

Construction began in early April 1960. Spokane Civil Defense Director Clyde H. Friend, Spokane County Civil Defense Director Clyde J. Chaffins, and Northwest Contract owner Burt Jesmore were among those present for the ground-breaking. Jesmore's firm completed the shelter in May 1960. Inland Empire Women's Civil Defense Council President Mrs. Raymond H. Grant (whose family home in England had been struck by a Nazi bomb during WWII) opened the shelter to the public at a ribbon-cutting ceremony May 24, 1960.[70]

After the ribbon festooned across the entrance to the shelter was cut, public visitors followed a cement path that ran across Vandervert's front yard and led to the shelter's entryway. A house door laid nearly flat against the ground and an air vent pipe protruding approximately two and a half feet from the top of the ground were all that Vandervert's guests could see of the shelter from aboveground. Beyond the door was a steep flight of stairs that visitors used to descend into the shelter. On the day of the opening, a *Spokane Daily Chronicle* photographer was among the public onlookers; he descended into the shelter and captured a shot of Burt Jesmore demonstrating the shelter's ventilation system by hand-cranking an air blower located between the top and lower roosts of a bunk bed. After the opening ceremony, Spokane's civil defense department invited the public to shelter viewings on Wednesdays and weekends. Press accounts of the shelter did not specify the details of Vandervert's contract with the national civil defense agency, but when the federal government gave a shelter to a homeowner in Everett, Washington, the deal had stipulated that the shelter had to stay open to the public for a year. Vandervert probably struck a similar bargain. By August 9, 1960, four hundred families had visited the demonstration shelter at Vandervert's home. On Sunday, October 1, 1961, six hundred people visited the shelter and set a record for the largest crowd to see the shelter in a single day.[71]

The large visitor tallies in the fall of 1961 indicated that the public took fallout protection seriously. Early adopters of backyard bunkers and basement hideaways, who might have been seen before as oddballs, were now vindicated. Kennedy had seemed to endorse private fallout shelters in his Berlin Crisis speech. Spokane's City Council sanctioned and encouraged home shelter construction by waiving building permit fees for the structures. In the November 19, 1961, letters section of the *Spokesman-Review*, Denton R. Vander Poel declared bombastically that the shelter craze had "hit Spokane like a megaton of bricks."[72]

Home Fallout Shelter Construction Companies, 1961

At least one zealous shelter salesman in Spokane uses the pitch that Spokane "is a hot spot" with its air bases and missile sites. Anyone who lives here without a shelter is a lunatic, is the sales talk he uses.

—Spokesman-Review

Shelter construction companies in Spokane sprang up to cater to the public's rising interest in fallout protection. The Spokane Civil Defense Department helped promote these private outfits. On October 9, 1961, Spokane Civil Defense Director Clyde H. Friend said, "When people call at our office or by telephone we give them a complete list of local contractors and manufacturers that are building fallout shelters."[73]

Twelve companies built fallout shelters in Spokane from 1960 to 1962. Survival Construction Inc., run by Ray Lancaster, Chris Roberts, and Don Price, was one of the earliest Spokane firms to become sensitive to what Lancaster described as "a need and desire for radiation shelters economically priced." They incorporated in October 1960 and made their headquarters at West 1115 Broadway. Lancaster and his colleagues built fallout shelters, sold fallout shelter equipment, and offered do-it-yourself shelter construction kits.[74]

Most of Spokane's fallout shelter companies leaped into business during the Berlin Crisis in 1961. Spokane reporter Joel Ream identified Atlas Fallout Shelters; American Fallout Shelters, Incorporated; and Bomb Shelters, Incorporated, as some of the firms that were "hastily organized" at this time.[75]

Figure 26 **Fairchild AFB pilot Maj. C.J. Agenbroad designed a shelter and Welk Brothers Metal Products built it and delivered it to his door at W 1022 Beacon. He is pictured finishing the shelter in September 1961. He planned to bury the shelter in his yard. (*Spokane Daily Chronicle*)**

It is not certain when National Construction entered the shelter building business. National, at 111 East Sprague, distinguished itself from its competitors by billing itself as the "Builder of Our Local Civil Defense Fallout Shelter Model," which seemed to indicate that it took part in constructing the federally financed demonstration fallout shelter in Curtis C. Vandervert's yard, but it is not entirely clear that was the case. On September 3, 1961, it advertised underground fallout shelters for "Nothing Down."[76]

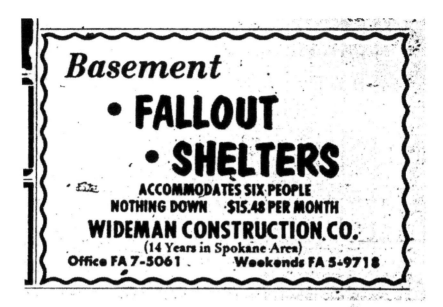

Figure 27 On Nov. 20, 1961, the Wideman Construction Company advertised shelters sold on a monthly installment plan. (*Spokane Daily Chronicle*)

More than half of the shelter contractors and shelter equipment suppliers had been established in other lines of work before the shelter craze struck, and they re-tailored their services and products (or sometimes just their advertising) to appeal to the surge of interest in shelters. In September 1961, Welk Brothers Metal Products built a family fallout shelter out of 10-gauge steel. On November 20, 1961, the Wideman Construction Company—a firm that claimed fourteen years of experience operating in Spokane—threw itself into the civil defense business by advertising that it could provide six-person basement fallout shelters. In October and November 1961, the Alaska Junk Company, which had sold blackout supplies to Spokanites during World War II, urged readers of the *Chronicle*'s classified section to shop at their Spokane store at East 3410 Desmet. "If you are building a Fallout Shelter and must KEEP COSTS DOWN," the company's ad said emphatically, "See Us for Pipe Fittings, Reinforcing Steel, Nails,

Steel Boxes, Steel Doors, Barrels, Pails, Tanks." The White Block Company at East 6219 Trent also promoted their supplies to the shelter building public.[77]

Shelter builders mostly crafted backyard bunkers and basement hideaways with concrete, steel, and cement block, but shelters were made of other materials, too. The Department of Defense Office of Civil Defense landed on the idea that a basement shelter could be built from a children's wading pool placed over wooden planks stacked atop shelves filled with books. There is no evidence that Spokane's shelter builders went that route, but they tried other novel approaches. The Sun Sales Corporation at Spokane Industrial Park designed and produced plastic fallout shelters. And on October 26, 1962, the Newton Lumber and Fuel Co. of North 1603 Belt, advertised "Survival Shelters of Laminated Wood." The company boasted that its wood shelters could "provide adequate fallout protection at a minimum cost" and were "warmer and more versatile" than other types of shelters.[78]

Figure 28   National Construction advertised on September 21, 1961. (*Spokesman-Review*)

Shelter sellers had to temper the extent of their claims or risk censure. The Federal Trade Commission oversaw shelter sellers, and Commission Chairman Paul Rand did not hesitate to warn the public that there were "fast-buck boys" in the shelter game. The Spokane Better Business Bureau kept an eye on shelter sellers, too. Spokane BBB Manager Mrs. Marie M. Ferrell testified in the shelter sellers' favor: "We haven't received a single complaint from anyone who has contracted to have a shelter built," and she assured residents, "We haven't had any drifters and fast-buck promoters trying to sell shelters here, either." In contrast to Ferrell's report, a Spokane newspaper alleged that one shelter seller went overboard in his pursuit of clients by melodramatically capitalizing on the public's fear of nuclear war. On November 19, 1961, the *Spokesman-Review* declared, "at least one zealous shelter salesman in Spokane uses the pitch that Spokane 'is a hot spot' with its air bases and missile sites. Anyone who lives here without a shelter is a lunatic, is the sales talk he uses."[79]

While a nuclear war scare could motivate buyers, shelter vendors could not stay in business by relying on war fears alone. To hawk its products, a shelter company had to make itself stand out, and it had to provide the public a reason to choose its firm over others. The flood of visitors to Vandervert's federally funded shelter had proved that people were drawn by an opportunity to examine an actual shelter. Three Spokane firms demonstrated that they appreciated this approach by building full-scale shelters to dramatically showcase their products to the public. While the Vandervert shelter might have provided inspiration, the companies were not content to simply mimic the federal project. Each offered a unique sales angle with its shelters. The American Fallout Shelter Company promised speedy construction to the public; the Spokane Culvert and Fabricating Company offered a prize; and the Fallout Bomb Shelter Center provided a spectacle.

Figure 29   Frank (in pipe) and Ben (to right) Stone show off
             their Spokane Culvert and Fabricating Company
             demonstration shelter in October 1961. The name
             of the welder on top of the shelter is unknown.
             (*Spokesman-Review*)

Figure 30   Jack Livingston and Edward Knakal ready the
             American Fallout Shelter, Inc. demonstration
             shelter in October 1961. (*Spokesman-Review*)

A trio of entrepreneurs formed the American Fallout Shelter Company in the early part of October 1961. Richard L. Salvesen, described by the *Spokesman-Review* as a "veteran home builder," was president of the firm; Jack Livingston served as vice president; and Edward Knakal was secretary-treasurer. From their headquarters at East 1518 Francis, they offered a range of fallout shelters in styles that could be scaled to meet an individual's needs and budget. On November 12, 1961, American advertised that it had "the latest underground model on display," which was "already a leading seller in the west." American's six-person shelter was made of concrete and steel, and the company promised that it came completely equipped and installed underground for only $1,573. It also boasted "maximum 3-day installations" for homeowners who wanted protection in a hurry.[80]

Thanks to their know-how from working on conventional steel projects, Ben G. Stone and Frank Stone, the operators of the Spokane Culvert and Fabricating Company at East 6212 Main, were able to offer the public corrugated-steel fallout shelters in the fall of 1961. To advertise their product, the Stones, in collaboration with Northtown shopping-area merchants who wanted to promote the grand opening of three Northtown stores, held a drawing to give away a "Civil Defense Approved" pre-fabricated fallout shelter stocked with survival supplies. The shelter was temporarily located between a food market and a department store on Wellesley. An advertisement for the drawing—scheduled to be held on October 21, 1961—promised that "the complete shelter and its displayed equipment will be delivered to the winner's home . . . ready for you to excavate and bury in your yard." No purchase was necessary to enter the drawing, but presumably the prize winner would have needed a yard and the resources to requisition a large hole in the ground.[81]

The Fallout Bomb Shelter Center (a division of Consolidated Western Contractors), headquartered at 2303 East Sprague, was the next Spokane company to build a demonstration shelter and boast about it. On November 3, 7, and 9, 1961, it advertised in Spokane newspapers that it had "fallout bomb shelters" on display at Shadle Center. The ads announced a unique attraction: "Your chance to see a family of 4 living in this completely equipped shelter." It was not clear from the advertisement whether the family was involved in a long term test of the shelter or simply occupying the shelter during business hours, serving as living mannequins. Even with that ambiguity (or perhaps because of it) the Fallout Bomb Shelter Center's advertising copy was intriguing.[82]

Whether Spokane shelter sellers employed fear-based sales tactics to capture business through the public's concern about the possibility of nuclear war or were merely creative with their advertising, they must have all felt confident about their prospects for success in the summer and fall of 1961. Similarly, they all must have been surprised when the public's interest in private shelters ended abruptly. In July 1962, Spokane reporter Kent Graybill looked back on the shelter "fad" and observed that it "died quicker than the hula-hoops."[83]

The End of the Private Shelter Fad, 1961–1962

Spokane's once burgeoning fallout shelter business has fallen on dark days.

—Joel Ream

As the 1961 Berlin Crisis highlighted the risk of nuclear war, and shelter sellers went to creative lengths to promote their products, another factor argued against the wide-spread adoption of home shelters: cost. Private fallout shelters were not the exclusive domain of the rich, but even the simplest shelters were still expensive. In Spokane, shelters belonging to Director Clyde H. Friend, Dewey Allsop, and Curtis Vandervert represented the spectrum of shelter costs. Director Clyde H. Friend claimed that his basement shelter had cost him only $306 to build. Vandervert's fallout shelter, which had been paid for by the federal government, was built by a contractor for $1,986. Dewey Allsop proved that a Spokane homeowner could construct an underground concrete shelter similar to the federal shelter in Vandervert's yard for approximately $700, but this accomplishment was possible because Allsop did most of the work on the shelter himself. According to Washington State Civil Defense Administration Director Charles C. Ralls, the prices of shelters varied greatly depending on what type of protection a homeowner sought. He informed Gene Farinet of NBC news on October 20, 1961: "Fabricated shelters range from $1,000 and up for reinforced concrete underground; from $1,800 and up for steel underground; and from $500 for wood fabrication above ground (covered with dirt) to $2,000 plus installed underground."[84]

The expense of private shelters led a pair of Spokanites to announce their support for public fallout shelters in the letters column of the *Spokesman-Review*. On May 1, 1961, Mrs. G. Miller of North 1712 Ash expressed concern about the high price of individual preparations to survive nuclear attack and asked, "Where are the public shelters?" L. B. Knisley of West 827 First complained that fallout shelters "should be a No. 1 program for our Department of Defense to protect all the people and not just those people who have the cash to build a shelter or have good credit."[85]

Phillip W. Amborn, a Spokane resident who was halfway in the midst of building a fallout shelter in the basement of his family's home at North 1420 Washington, also rallied for the cause of public shelters. Amborn was among a group of Spokanites who corresponded with Washington's Sen. Henry M. Jackson to express support for government assistance to widen the availability of public and private shelters. Amborn feared what might happen if there were not enough shelters available in the event of a nuclear war. "Those with shelters," he predicted, "would be stormed by those without them and death would probably ensue from struggles for possession of the shelters as much as from fallout. There would be no law except that of self-survival."[86]

Sen. Jackson had his own concerns about the nation's shelter posture. On November 8, 1961, Jackson cautioned students at Eastern Washington State College in Cheney, Washington, "It would be disastrous to present an image to the world of being in our backyard digging holes in which to hide from the Russians." Two days later, the Senator added to his remark: "I cannot see any value in building a special shelter which could be used one time and one time only." He conceded that cheap basement shelters were fine, and he spoke in favor of surveying buildings to identify spaces in existing buildings that could serve as public fallout shelters. Ultimately, he objected to costlier public or private shelter proposals. "If the majority of families in this country suddenly spent what would amount to billions of dollars on fallout shelters," Jackson predicted, "Khrushchev would announce immediately that the Soviet Union is prepared to retaliate against any aggression with bacteriological or chemical warfare. Against this type of an attack, a fallout shelter would be no defense at all." Jackson even called into question whether any type of shelter would be worthwhile by forecasting that Spokane would have only ten minutes warning before an attack, which might not allow many people to reach shelters before the Soviet bombs and missiles exploded. Even if people made it to the shelters before the city was struck, Jackson doubted the shelters could do much good against nuclear blasts.[87]

Figure 31   **Backyard bunker. Perhaps in response to earlier criticism of the high cost of shelters, the federal government suggested "low-cost backyard fallout shelters" in 1966. (Department of Defense, Office of Civil Defense, *Personal and Family Survival*)**

Figure 32   Basement hideaway. This "improvised basement shelter" was one of the federal government's economical civil defense suggestions in 1966. (Department of Defense, Office of Civil Defense, *Personal and Family Survival*)

Jackson's criticism undercut Spokane's elected officials, civil defense authorities, and construction firms who were promoting backyard bunkers and basement hideaways. Jackson's remarks also spurred members of the public to write to the *Spokesman-Review* and vent their opposition to all types of shelters. "Our first energies," Mrs. June G. Potter lectured, "should be directed against the Communist conspiracy. Too many of us think there is nothing we can do except dig a hole." Mrs. Lena Butler added, "God forbid that we be placed in the same category as rats and moles." Mrs. Walter Senters urged Spokanites to make some efforts to secure peace. She asked, "Can't we express hope instead of so much fear?" After surveying the shelter construction in Spokane, she chided the city, declaring, "Our children deserve better than this."[88]

As the danger of the Berlin Crisis appeared to ease, Spokanites went along with the rest of the United States public and reduced their patronage of shelter vendors to the point where they had effectively vetoed the private shelter idea with their pocketbooks. On July 8, 1962, *Spokesman-Review* observer Joel Ream declared, "Spokane's once burgeoning fallout shelter business has fallen on dark days." According to Ream, Frank Stone, of the Spokane Culvert & Fabricating Company, looked at his inventory of unsold pre-fabricated steel fallout shelters and confessed, "I don't know what we'll ever do with them." Stone added, "I think about every culvert plant in the country has half a dozen of these against the back fence."[89]

Stone was correct when he speculated that hard times for shelter sellers extended beyond the radius of Spokane. On May 6, 1962, the Associated Press reported that in Washington State "the home fallout shelter boom has virtually fizzled out." Shelter businesses collapsed all over the United States.[90]

"Interest is lagging now," Spokane County Civil Defense Director Clyde J. Chaffins admitted, "but let someone shoot off another superbomb and they'll come flocking in again for information." As Chaffins predicted, a nuclear crisis revived the public's appetite for shelters. The revival was caused by President Kennedy's announcement that the United States had discovered Soviet nuclear missiles stationed in Cuba. Vexingly for shelter contractors, the crisis did not stimulate Spokane's moribund private shelter industry. Instead, the Cuban Missile Crisis of October 1962 lifted the curtain on the awkward first act of the country's public fallout shelter program.[91]

VI. Public Fallout Shelters, 1961–1978

What is it that we ought to do for the population in affected areas, in case the bombs go off? Is there something we can do?

—President John F. Kennedy

City of Spokane Civil Defense Director Clyde H. Friend testified that during the Cuban Missile Crisis his office received "thousands of calls" from worried Spokanites "who wanted to know where shelter was, any shelter so that the chances of survival for themselves and their loved ones would be increased." The assault on Friend's phone lines began after President Kennedy told American television and radio audiences on October 22, 1962, that the Soviet Union was building "offensive missile sites" in Cuba. "The purpose of these bases," Kennedy explained, "can be none other than to provide a nuclear strike capability against the Western Hemisphere." Spokane sat beyond the reach of the farthest-flying Soviet missiles that could have been launched from Cuba, but the city was still in peril because the stand-off over the missiles could have escalated into an all-out nuclear war. According to historian Duane Colt Denfeld, the Atlas nuclear missiles based around Spokane were re-targeted from Russia to point toward Cuba during the 1962 crisis. Soviet missiles armed with nuclear warheads were likely already targeted at Spokane, and long-range bombers based in northern Russia were a short distance from Spokane and could have reached the city easily by way of a quick flight over the North Pole.[92]

In the face of this potential atomic exchange, Civil Defense Director Clyde H. Friend told reporters that his switchboard was "lit up like a Christmas tree." The callers must have been disappointed by the response they received. Friend told callers that the buildings in Spokane suitable as public fallout shelters were not marked because the signs from the federal government had not yet arrived. He advised, "stock a shelter; be prepared to evacuate; then do as you are told according to the warning signal" and the emergency broadcasting network on AM radio. The Spokane County Civil Defense office told its callers that the shelter options in the county were just as limited as those in the city. "Do the best with what you have at home," the county instructed, "the public shelters are not yet ready in county areas and there is no place to go on your own."[93]

The Cuban Missile Crisis arrived as leaders of the nation's public fallout shelter program were attempting to provide public shelters for 50 million Americans by surveying, licensing, stocking, and marking fallout shelter spaces in existing buildings. Civil defense leaders in Spokane and the rest of the United States were nowhere close to reaching this ambitious goal when the Cuban crisis spurred the public to inquire about the progress of the shelter system. By September 30, 1962, the national fallout shelter survey had identified 1,286 facilities in Washington State that offered a radiation protection factor of 100 or more, yet by the October Crisis, only 267 of those structures had been licensed as fallout shelters. The national picture was no better. On October 25, 1962, the Associated Press reported, based on sources in the Defense Department, that the United States could protect only a few hundred thousand people in public shelters and that none of the shelters were stocked with survival supplies.[94]

The day after President Kennedy announced the Cuban Missile Crisis to the public, as Spokane callers reached the city and county civil defense offices to ask about the availability of public fallout shelters, Kennedy held a similar conversation with Assistant Secretary of Defense for Civil Defense Steuart Pittman, who lamented that the public fallout shelter program was not ready for service. Kennedy was contemplating invading Cuba to attack the Soviet missiles stationed there, and he was concerned about the consequences to the American public if the invasion caused the Soviets to launch their missiles on the island at the United States. "Can we, maybe before we invade," the President wondered, "evacuate these cities?" Pittman answered, "If we knew that there would be no nuclear response, it might make some sense. If there will be fallout, the only protection that exists today is in the cities, and there's little or no protection in the rural areas." Still searching for a solution, the President queried, "What is it that we ought to do for the population in affected areas, in case the bombs go off? Is there something we can do?" Pittman suggested that they could speed up the public fallout shelter program.[95]

Following Kennedy's conversation with Pittman, the U.S. government initiated two shortcuts to increase the nation's inventory of public fallout shelters. The government gave civil defense officials temporary permission to do away with written agreements when establishing public fallout shelters and allowed them to rely on oral permissions instead. The government also lowered the minimum protection factor for public shelter spaces from 100 to 40. More might have been done to accelerate the public shelter program if the Cuban Missile Crisis had not ended on October 28, 1962.[96]

To end the crisis, the Soviets consented to remove their missiles from Cuba in exchange for a pledge from Kennedy that he would not invade Cuba and a secret tacit understanding that the U.S. would remove its nuclear missiles stationed near the Soviet border in Turkey. With the end of the world averted by diplomacy, civil defense leaders continued preparing public fallout shelters so that they could answer the public more effectively if another crisis were to trigger the nation's fears about nuclear war and citizens were to inquire again about the availability of public fallout shelters.[97]

Establishing Public Fallout Shelters, 1961–1969

Spokane thus becomes the first city in the state to have more shelter spaces than population.

—Spokane Daily Chronicle

Prior to the Cuban Missile Crisis of 1962, the day after President Kennedy's Berlin Crisis speech of 1961, Secretary of Defense Robert McNamara successfully leveraged the President's powerful oration to pry $207.6 million from Congress to establish a public fallout shelter system in the United States. The work called for surveying potential public shelter space in existing buildings, licensing the shelter spaces by obtaining agreements from building owners that would allow the shelter spaces to be used by the public in an emergency, stocking the shelters with food and other survival supplies, and marking the shelter spaces with signs to alert the public. McNamara's Department of Defense assigned the Northwest and Alaskan Division of the Navy's Bureau of Yards and Docks to complete the public fallout shelter survey of Washington State. The Bureau of Yards and Docks tackled the job county-by-county with assistance from the Seattle and Walla Walla Districts of the U.S. Army Corps of Engineers. The Seattle District of the U.S. Army Corps of Engineers oversaw the survey of Spokane County and negotiated a contract with the Spokane architectural-engineering firm Culler, Gale, Martell, Norrie and Davis to handle the ground work.[98]

The survey of Spokane began in the winter of 1961 when Kenneth P. Norrie and Walter Z. Davis led a four-man team that scoured Spokane County to discover potential spaces for establishing public fallout shelters. Norrie and Davis had prepared to conduct the survey by studying fallout shelter analysis and design in a Department of Defense Office of Civil Defense-sponsored course taught at the University of Washington. By the summer of 1964, 209 architects and engineers in Washington State had graduated from fallout shelter analysis courses. The classes taught students to design fallout shelters from scratch and to modify existing structures to improve their shelter capabilities. To the benefit of architects and engineers such as Norrie and Davis slated to survey potential fallout shelters, the courses also taught students to identify existing structures that could serve as effective fallout shelters without any need for improvements.[99]

After their shelter schooling was complete, Norrie and Davis combed Spokane for potential safe havens from fallout. The *Spokesman-Review* reported in December 1961 that Norrie and Davis were "studying buildings, tunnels, mine shafts and other structures which could be used in event of nuclear attack." If Norrie and Davis followed the basic fallout shelter survey procedure recommended by the Department of Defense Office of Civil Defense, they studied every Spokane County building and structure they thought might work as a public fallout shelter, noting the address, owner, and purpose. They would have also recorded construction materials while measuring dimensions and the thicknesses of the walls and roof to calculate a protection factor (PF), the degree to which a shelter could protect its occupants from radiation.[100]

Estimating a shelter's exact PF, appears to have been a complicated task. A 1960 *Fallout Shelter Surveys: Guide for Architects and Engineers*, published by the Office of Civil and Defense Mobilization, required shelter analysts to fill out ten pages of forms, consult six pages of charts and two pages of tables, and run formulas to determine the protection factor of a single shelter. By 1962, this process was operating differently. Under the management of the Office of Civil Defense, located within Robert McNamara's Department of Defense, who inherited shelter survey responsibilities from the OCDM, architects and engineers collected shelter measurements and sent them to the DOD for computer analysis. The Department of Defense Office of Civil Defense boasted that when the computer analyzed a card it took "less than ten seconds" to calculate its results while "a competently trained architect and engineer would take as much as ten hours to perform the same type of analysis."[101]

Thanks to the initial survey work of Norrie and Davis and the calculating speed of the DOD's computer, Civil Defense Director Clyde H. Friend was able to announce on October 5, 1962, that the Spokane County fallout shelter survey had been completed. The survey determined that Spokane County had 155 buildings suitable for sheltering a total of 382,900 people. Friend didn't announce the protection factor for each structure, but he claimed they were all 100 or greater, so that a person inside a shelter would receive at least 100 times less radiation than a person outside. Additional surveys conducted by the U.S. Army Corps of Engineers in 1964 and 1969 brought the total number of buildings in Spokane eligible to serve as public fallout shelters at least as high as 249. The surveys identified suitable locations for public fallout shelters in a range of buildings: offices, factories, apartments, hotels, motels, retirement homes, churches, parking garages, stores, shopping malls, a funeral home, schools, libraries, bakeries, airports, a power station, and the launch operations building of a decommissioned Atlas nuclear missile base. Since the U.S. government lowered its minimum standard for the protection factors of fallout shelters from 100 to 40 during the Cuban Missile Crisis, the buildings that were added to Spokane's shelter inventory after 1962 may have offered less shielding from gamma radiation than the buildings identified in the earlier survey.

Identifying a building that could work as a public fallout shelter was not equivalent to securing a property owner's permission to use that building as a public fallout shelter. The Department of Defense Office of Civil Defense gave city and county governments the job of petitioning property owners to agree to allow their buildings to be enrolled in the public fallout shelter program. By June 26, 1963, Spokane area civil defense authorities had convinced the owners of 106 buildings in Spokane and Spokane County to allow space in their buildings to be designated as public fallout shelters. Thanks to additional owner permission agreements, the number of buildings in the Spokane area public fallout shelter network ballooned to 249 by 1969.[102]

Building owners who signed public shelter licensing agreements were eligible to receive emergency supplies from the federal government, as long as the owners made no plans to bar people from entering the shelters based on "race, religion, or color." The federally supplied shelter provisions included food, drinking water containers, sanitation kits, medical supplies, and devices to measure radiation. The Department of Defense Office of Civil Defense made local civil defense groups responsible for transporting these goods from government warehouses to eligible public shelters. By March 31, 1970, civil defense authorities had stashed emergency supplies in 102,805 public fallout shelters in the United States.[103]

Spokane's city civil defense workers, with help from community volunteers, began moving federally provided supplies from a civil defense warehouse at the Spokane Industrial Park into Spokane public fallout shelters in May 1963. By November 5, 1963, they had loaded supplies into 81 city shelters—including a very large shelter established in the downtown Bon Marche department store (bought by Macy's in 2003). Civil defense officials estimated that 12,938 people could be sheltered in the

Bon in the event of nuclear war. To provision this prospective horde, civil defense volunteers crowded the fake-cactus store displays and Valentine's Day decorations in the store's sub-basement with 2,700 seventeen and a half–gallon-sized water cans and an undisclosed amount of other survival supplies.[104]

After stocking the Bon, Spokane city civil defense authorities continued provisioning public shelters. On August 20, 1964, Director Friend announced that 110 fallout shelters in Spokane had been stocked with emergency supplies that could sustain 82,800 people for fourteen days. On January 6, 1965, Friend announced that public shelters in 132 Spokane buildings were stocked with emergency supplies worth $213,801. By the time Spokane officials stocked the Spokane YMCA on Havermale Island with survival supplies on February 28, 1967, the YMCA numbered among 176 fallout shelters in Spokane that had been equipped to sustain 187,770 people in the event of a nuclear war. Since Spokane's population was 186,770, the *Spokane Daily Chronicle* trumpeted, "Spokane thus becomes the first city in the state to have more shelter spaces than population."[105]

President Kennedy made it clear that the federal government would feed people who took to public shelters in an emergency, but the menu in the shelters was initially a mystery. Residents of Spokane following Congressional hearings on the fallout shelter program, might have begun to worry about the doomsday cuisine when Secretary of Defense Robert S. McNamara disclosed to the Military Operations Subcommittee of the House Committee on Government Operations that the public shelters were going to be stocked with "austere emergency rations." During McNamara's August 1, 1961, testimony, he warned Congress members, "Consumption of this ration by some persons may involve some discomfort." In a December 1961 Kennedy-era pamphlet that taught the public "what to know and do about nuclear attack," the Department of Defense Office of Civil Defense advised public shelter dwellers to supplement the federally provided shelter fare with "familiar foods" brought from home because they would be "more heartening and acceptable during times of stress." Unappetizingly, the final sentence in the pamphlet's section about food advised, "In an emergency, *most* canned and packaged animal foods can be eaten by humans without harm [emphasis added]."[106]

The suspense about the type of food to be stocked in public shelters ended when the federal government revealed that it planned to serve crackers. Between 1962 and 1964, the federal government spent $70.4 million to buy 165,000 tons of survival crackers. On June 29, 1965, Friend declared that Spokane's fallout shelters were stocked with enough survival crackers to provide each shelter occupant with 900 calories a day for fourteen days. Some of the crackers stocked in Spokane's shelters were made from wheat flour and others were made from bulgur. Spokane newspaper journalist Don Rice sampled the fallout shelter rations and reported that "those crackers tasted like pie crust without salt, sugar or cinnamon." Director Friend conceded, "the shelter food rations need to be supplemented to really enjoy eating." In addition, Friend acknowledged, "They are very dry and encourage thirst."[107]

To quench the thirst of cracker-parched shelter dwellers, the Department of Defense Office of Civil Defense commissioned container manufacturers to produce metal cans to store water in shelters. The manufacturers made the water cans sixteen inches in diameter and twenty-one inches tall and rated them to hold seventeen and a half gallons of liquid. Civil defense workers moved the water cans into the shelters when they were empty and filled them with water from a hose. When a can was filled with water, it weighed 150 pounds.[108]

A supply of water in the public shelters was essential for choking down dry survival crackers, and it would also aid sanitation. "In the limited space of a shelter," the Department of Defense Office of Civil Defense warned, "good sanitation is not merely a matter of comfort, it could be a matter of life and death." If sanitation in the shelters broke down, public shelter occupants would face the risks of contracting typhoid, dysentery, and other sicknesses. With an awareness of these hazards, the federal government announced in May 1962 that it had hired seven workshops for the blind to produce a total of 849,996 sanitation kits for use in public fallout shelters. Workshops in Arizona, Maryland, Missouri, New York, North Carolina, and Ohio took seventeen and a half–gallon capacity "fibre drums" and packed them with cleaning chemicals, toilet paper, and fourteen other sanitary items that shelterees could use to keep a tidy hideaway. One of the most thoughtful items in the sanitation kit was a toilet seat. Shelter dwellers could combine the seat with an empty water can to create a commode.[109]

Since the shelter accommodations were crude, occupants might wonder how soon after a nuclear attack they could venture outside. Civil defense officials stocked radiation measuring devices in the shelters to help shelterees determine when fallout levels outside were low enough to allow them to leave the shelters safely. It is not clear what specific models of radiation measuring devices were stocked in Spokane's shelters, but federal civil defense pamphlets indicated that public shelters were equipped with two main types: dosimeters and ratemeters. Pen-shaped dosimeters were designed to be clipped to a person's clothing to keep track of the total amount of radiation the person received. Ratemeters were intended to allow shelter denizens to monitor when levels of radiation outside the shelter were low enough to allow people to leave. In August 1964, Director Friend told the *Spokane Daily*

Chronicle that Spokane's public fallout shelter supplies included radiation measuring equipment but he did not give any specific details about it.[110]

No matter how carefully shelter occupants monitored radiation levels, they would likely face the risk of radiation poisoning, conventional illnesses, and injuries. To enable shelter occupants to render first aid care, the DOD's Office of Civil Defense provided medical supplies to Spokane civil defense authorities to stock in public fallout shelters. The medical kits included common first aid supplies such as rubbing alcohol, aspirin tablets, ear drops, diarrhea medication, and laxative tablets. The medical kits also included phenobarbital sedative pills. In a booklet of instructions the Department of Defense Office of Civil Defense included with the boxes of shelter medical supplies, the department advised shelter managers to administer the phenobarbital, under the guidance of trained medical professionals, to "persons whose tensions present an emotional problem affecting other shelter occupants." The booklet also suggested that the phenobarbital tablets should be given to anyone who was suffering from coughs, pain, abdominal cramps, convulsions, severe nausea, or insomnia.[111]

On top of the supplies furnished by the federal government, some of Spokane's public shelters may have been outfitted with housewarming gifts from the Society of Gideons and the Veterans of Foreign Wars. In February 1965, W. T. Grimmer of the Spokane Chapter of the Society of Gideons—the organization responsible for putting bibles in the bedside bureaus at many hotels and motels—gave 130 Bibles to Spokane Mayor Neal R. Fosseen with the intention that the Bibles should be stocked in Spokane's public fallout shelters. In October 1967, Spokane's Hillyard Post of the V.F.W. (Post 1474) gave 250 miniature flags to the Spokane city civil defense organization to add to the essential supplies in the city's fallout shelters. The donation of the flags earned the Spokane V.F.W. post the Bronze Award of Merit from the national board of the V.F.W., who called the action "a fine example of the patriotic work being done by the VFW throughout the nation." Newspaper accounts documented the donations of the Bibles and flags, but Spokane's two largest papers did not report whether Spokane officials actually distributed the Bibles and flags to Spokane's public fallout shelters.[112]

Figure 33   If Spokane officials ever wanted to swear up and down on a stack of bibles that fallout shelters worked, this was their chance. The Spokane Gideons gifted 130 bibles to Spokane's public fallout shelters. In this picture, W. T. Grimmer of the Gideons (left) hands Mayor Fosseen (right) a bible while Civil Defense Director Friend watches the hand-off. (*Spokesman-Review*)

Figure 34 **Spokane Civil Defense Director Clyde H. Friend (left) and Spokane Mayor Neal R. Fosseen marked city hall as a public fallout shelter with the distinctive sign above on November 27, 1962. (*Spokane Daily Chronicle*)**

To make sure that Americans could identify public fallout shelters, the federal government ordered 400,000 metal fallout shelter signs for eighty-nine cents a piece in 1962. The signs were emblazoned with a logo of three yellow triangles clustered inside a circle of black that sat on a field of yellow. The words "FALLOUT SHELTER" were printed below the logo. On January 2, 1967, Spokane's Civil Defense Department reported that it had marked 175 Spokane public fallout shelters with these signs. By hanging the signs, Spokane civil defense workers advertised that the public shelters were surveyed, licensed, loaded with supplies, and ready to occupy in the event of a nuclear war.[113]

"Man, Some Bomb-Shelter Test," 1967

Man, some bomb-shelter test!

—Spokane teenager

After Spokane's public fallout shelters had been stocked with emergency supplies and sign-posted, they were ready for use by the public, but civil defense leaders wondered whether the public was ready for the shelters. To answer that question, Spokane's Civil Defense Department asked community volunteers to take part in a public fallout shelter habitability test. Seventy-eight members of the public stepped forward—or, rather, stepped down—to participate. In an arrangement reminiscent of a youth's accepting a dare to spend a night locked inside a haunted house, the volunteers agreed to spend twenty-nine hours isolated inside a basement shelter located in Spokane's Water Department Auditorium at East 914 Grace.

Civil defense officials asked shelter test participants to imagine they were under a nuclear attack. To help the shelterees stay focused on trying to survive the make-believe nuclear war, civil defense workers confiscated radios belonging to the test participants and prohibited the volunteers from making phone calls. As civil defense officials closed the shelter door and began the exercise on March 11, 1967, Tom Curtiss, a Spokane city civil defense aide, spoke ominously to a reporter loitering outside the entrance to the basement shelter, "These people, as of this moment, are cut off from the world."[114]

Before the 1967 test, only a few Spokane residents had ever sequestered themselves in a fallout shelter in such a public fashion. A family of four had taken up residence in a shelter located at a Shadle Center store parking lot in November 1961 to promote area businesses and advertise a shelter seller in Spokane called the Fallout Bomb Shelter Center. In a different promotional venture, newlyweds may have nested in a demonstration fallout shelter at the 1961 Spokane Home Show. Washington State Civil Defense Director Charles Ralls and Spokane Civil Defense Director Clyde Friend corresponded in October 1961 to arrange "the promotional plan for a honeymoon couple to stay in a shelter for a period of nine days at the Spokane Home Show." Despite the evidence of this planning, no documents or newspaper stories ever surfaced to confirm whether the civil defense directors enacted their plan to turn a fallout shelter at the home show into a honeymoon suite.[115]

The idea of a honeymoon type of stay in a public fallout shelter during a nuclear war would have seemed unlikely to sociologists and psychologists who appeared at the National Academy of Sciences' "Symposium on Human Problems in the Utilization of Fallout Shelters" held in Washington, D.C., in February 1960. At the gathering, sociologists and psychologists who specialized in studying social dynamics in cramped living quarters painted a grim picture of the experience people might expect to have while living in a public fallout shelter. John H. Rohrer, a professor of psychology at Georgetown University Medical School, presented a paper called "Implications for Fallout Shelter Living from Studies of Submarine Habitability and Adjustment to Polar Isolation." Rohrer assumed that the shelters would provide adequate food, air, water, and temperature for survival. In Rohrer's estimate, however, people were the weakest link in the shelter system. He characterized public shelter dwellers as likely to be senseless, fickle-headed bigots. "It is probable that, under shelter isolation conditions, most of the deprivations," he predicted, "will revolve around those superficial to physical survival; e.g., deprivations felt over missing a TV show, not having hot meals, not having sufficient privacy or a space that one can call one's own, or complaints growing out of racial or religious prejudices." Rohrer's prediction about problems with prejudices was echoed by Delbert C. Miller, a professor of sociology at Indiana University who studied living conditions at isolated radar bases. Miller perceived that "the allocation of limited food or water might be especially amenable to discriminatory practices."[116]

In contrast to the grim remarks of the psychologists and sociologists at the national sciences symposium, behavioral science specialists at the American Institute for Research (A.I.R.) in Pittsburgh concluded that groups of thirty people could easily manage to get-along together during long stays in fallout shelters. The federal Office of Civil and Defense Mobilization commissioned the A.I.R. to oversee three experiments in which three groups of thirty people spent a week together in a fallout shelter. The A.I.R. also conducted a fourth experiment in which thirty people spent two weeks in a fallout shelter. The scientists found that all four groups survived their shelter trials with minimal complaints. In two of the experiments, the scientists employed shelter managers to look after the groups and discovered that "trained and designated managers increased the overall adjustment to shelter living."[117]

The Department of Defense Office of Civil Defense, perhaps taking a cue from A.I.R.'s findings, trained volunteers to act as public shelter managers in cities across the United States. The federal agency educated Spokane Fire Captain Lloyd F. Bloomington (the coordinator of fire services for the City of Spokane's Civil Defense Department) in shelter management at a civil defense school in Alameda, California. Bloomington agreed in February 1964 to share his training with thirty City of Spokane employees who would serve as managers for public fallout shelters located in buildings owned by the city. Thanks to Bloomington's efforts, and perhaps the work of other unknown trainers, Spokane had seventy qualified fallout shelter managers by March 25, 1964.[118]

In 1967, when Spokane civil defense officials launched the public shelter test, they gained a chance to demonstrate shelter management practices in action. Coast Guard Chief Petty Officer Robert C. Cookson acted as the shelter manager during the exercise. Cookson's rule lasted from the start of the test at 10:00 a.m. on Saturday March 11, 1967, to the end of the trial at 3:00 p.m. on March 12. In the Spokane Water Department Auditorium's 108 feet x 36 feet basement fallout shelter, Cookson supervised eight nuns, thirty-six other females, and thirty-four males. Of the entire group, which ranged in age from six to fifty-five, forty-one were teenagers.[119]

Brad Smith, one of the teenagers who participated in the shelter experiment, wrote about his experience for the Gonzaga Preparatory School newspaper, the *Gonzagan*. Smith related that civil defense officials began the test by herding the volunteers into the shelter to the sound of a blaring air raid siren. Once inside the shelter, civil defense officials read aloud fake news bulletins that described a nuclear attack on Spokane. "We were told," Smith reported, "that Spokane was being badly damaged by many bombs." To underscore this scenario, civil defense officials cut the lights in the shelter and advised the shelter guests that bombs had knocked out the city's power. A short while later, civil defense officials turned the lights back on.[120]

In the dimness of the simulated power outage, Smith could have bumped into fellow journalist Don Rice, a *Spokane Daily Chronicle* reporter who took part in the shelter test with his wife and four children. Rice wrote a story about the test and revealed to his readers that civil defense officials had tried to add drama to the shelter drill by asking shelter occupants to take turns standing guard at the basement doors. The guards were, in Rice's words, "to prevent outsiders from overcrowding the shelter's limited facilities and insiders from getting into the lethal world outside."

With the volunteers ensconced inside the basement, civil defense officials turned them into a captive audience and performance troupe. Officials asked the test participants to play-act how they might react to hypothetical emergencies that included a person in the shelter suffering death from exposure to radiation, a shelter occupant going insane, and a teenager fainting. Amid the role-playing, the shelter denizens were called upon to respond to a real emergency. A nun caught her veil in the shelter's air blower. Rice reported "she escaped with nothing more than a torn veil and bumped forehead."[121]

For added realism, civil defense leaders dished up the very foods that were stocked in Spokane's shelters and fed them to the shelter participants. "Our meals," Smith tallied in his *Gonzagan* article, "consisted of two crackers, four pieces of candy, and one glass of water." In slight disagreement, Rice explained in his *Spokane Daily Chronicle* article that shelter test volunteers were "allowed for each meal eight survival crackers, four pieces of 'carbohydrate supplement' that looked and tasted exactly like hard candy, plus six plastic glasses of distilled water (total, one quart) per day." It is not clear why Rice reported receiving more rations than Smith—Rice may have received portions that were reserved for adults or he could have counted the rations received by his entire family. Regardless of the exact portion sizes, it is evident that Rice was not pleased with his meals in the shelter. He described the crackers as flavorless and explained that "toward the end they were eaten only under the duress of real hunger."[122]

To educate the shelter occupants and keep them entertained, civil defense leaders showed films about radiation and nuclear weapons. Some teenagers in the shelter reclaimed their radios that had been confiscated by civil defense authorities and created their own amusement. The radios blared music in the evening, and the kids inaugurated what Rice described as "a swinging dance-fest." According to Rice, "One youth, with cute chick tenderly in arms, rhapsodized, 'Man, some bomb-shelter test!'"[123]

When the shelter test ended, shelter manager Cookson declared, "It all turned out well, with no fisticuffs or angry words. The most serious difficulty was when some of the teenagers had their radios on too loud."[124]

Prior to the shelter test, Director Friend had said that his organization was conducting the exercise to evaluate emergency preparedness plans and shelter management training and also "to prove that groups of strangers can live together for an extended period, under adverse conditions and with a minimum of supplies." The test met two of the goals Friend had outlined for it: testing emergency preparations and shelter management skills. However, the test did not completely satisfy Friend's goal "to prove that groups of strangers can live together for an extended period, under adverse conditions and with a minimum of supplies." Considering that civil defense officials had estimated that, in the event of a nuclear war, shelter dwellers would have had to stay hidden from outside radiation for as long as two weeks, one night in a shelter was not proof of the viability of an extended shelter stay.[125] Spokane residents probably got a better picture of what life in a public fallout shelter would have been like when a vicious ice storm in 1996 downed power lines and cut off electricity to tens of thousands of homes forcing hundreds of citizens to encamp at Red Cross shelters. The *Spokesman-Review* discovered twenty-two elderly shelter occupants suffered "a condition mental health workers called 'shelter shock'—a state of extreme mental agitation that causes disorientation and rising blood pressure."[126]

Despite its short duration, the 1967 test proved that, along with the fact that teens enjoy loud music, nearly a hundred Spokanites were interested in public fallout shelters as late as 1967. In addition, the exercise may have kindled a curiosity about shelters among the people who had merely read about it. Director Friend said that after the test, his office received "more inquiries than usual about civil defense." If Friend's callers asked where they could find public fallout shelters, as they had during the Cuban Missile Crisis, Friend could rattle off a list of more than two-hundred locations, which he had not been able to do in 1962. Even better, Friend could promise callers that he would soon send them a public fallout shelter utilization plan that featured maps of all the public shelters in Spokane and Spokane County. Unfortunately for Friend, the plan was the last hoorah for Spokane's public fallout shelters before the public and officials alike determined that the whole shelter endeavor was a hyperbolic charade.[127]

The Shelter Map and Plan, 1969

Be sure your family has studied this plan. It could save your life!

—*Community Shelter Plan*

The *Community Shelter Plan for Spokane and Spokane County* debuted in mailboxes of Spokane County in November 1969. Prior to the plan's mailing, Wayne Carlson, a reporter for the *Spokane Daily Chronicle*, had explained to his readers that the *Community Shelter Plan* would answer the question of what to do when "you're home in bed. It's midnight. You're awakened by a siren, so you snap on a radio. You learn the country has been attacked by a nuclear bomb." True to Carlson's word, the one-page, double-sided, 35" X 23" *Community Shelter Plan* that arrived in mailboxes featured maps of public fallout shelter locations and encouraged Spokanites to create a "family emergency plan" that would "tell each member of the family where to go and what to do in case of nuclear attack."[128]

The creation of the plan was a gift from the Department of Defense Office of Civil Defense, who by June 30, 1970, had footed the bill for local governments to draw maps of public shelter locations and funded the distribution of these maps in shelter plans for 955 communities across the United States. The DOD's Office of Civil Defense assigned the U.S. Army Corps of Engineers to commission the Spokane Planning Department to create the Spokane area plan in 1967. Spokane Planning Director Vaughn P. Call took charge of the project by leading a sixty-seven-member policy advisory council and a twenty-eight-member technical committee that carried the plan to print.[129]

The plan gave Spokane residents the locations of 249 public fallout shelters so that people seemed to have a defense against fallout wherever they might roam. A new-born infant whose first cries mingled with the screams of the city's air raid sirens could be delivered to the protection of a shelter since Deaconess Hospital, and the rest of Spokane's major medical facilities, all had public fallout shelters. Students at most of Spokane's elementary schools, junior high schools, high schools, and colleges had shelters available on their campuses. Spokane workers had access to shelters at many job sites. Shoppers had access to public shelters at the Bon Marche, J.C. Penney's, Woolworth's, and the Crescent. A senior citizen who had opted to lodge at the Bethany Old Peoples Home or the Hawthorne Manor retirement community would find a public fallout shelter at both locations. Fallout shelters even cropped up at the Spokane Casket Company, the Smith Funeral Home, and Riverside Cemetery.[130]

The great number and diverse locations of Spokane area public fallout shelters gave readers of the *Community Shelter Plan* the impression that residents would have fallout protection that would follow them from the cradle to the grave, but the plan measured protection in arbitrary terms.

In the first year of their work, an obstacle became apparent to the civil defense strategists. "Our shelters are primarily in the downtown area," Spokane Planning Director Vaughan P. Call observed in February 1967. "Most of them are concentrated in the business district. You couldn't get enough people to them in the required time." Friend defined the window of time in which Spokane citizens had to make it to shelters in July 1967 when he announced that Spokane would have fifteen minutes of warning prior to a nuclear attack and thirty minutes after an attack before the city would be struck by fallout.[131]

Figure 35   The 1969 *Community Shelter Plan* showcased Spokane's progress in establishing public fallout shelters since Kennedy kicked off the program in 1961 with his Berlin Crisis speech. In this detail from the map section, the circled numbers and alphanumeric designators corresponded to an index that listed the address, or addresses, of one, or more, nearby fallout shelters available for use by the public in the event of a nuclear war. (*Community Shelter Plan*)

The Planning Department estimated that within Friend's forty-five minute countdown to radioactive landfall, twenty-seven percent of the city's population would not be able to make it to shelters in time to avoid deadly radiation because they lived too far away from downtown.[132]

Rather than establishing more shelters outside downtown, the Community Shelter Plan Advisory Committee papered over the problem of getting people to safety by lengthening the time they predicted citizens would have to find shelter from forty-five minutes to seventy-five minutes. They figured that this adjustment would allow them to class 30,000 more people as residents who lived within reachable distance of a designated public fallout shelter. The Advisory Committee added this time-table to the final printed version of the *Community Shelter Plan*, which advised readers, "If a nuclear attack should occur, you may have 75 minutes from the first warning to get from wherever you are (at home, at the office, at school, etc.) to a building that is marked as providing fallout protection."[133]

The gerrymandered time estimates in the final printed edition of the *Community Shelter Plan* hid the planners own uncertainty about whether people in the Spokane area would be able to run to shelters in time to beat the arrival of nuclear fallout. The plan itself hid the planners' unexamined assumption that Spokane would escape a direct nuclear strike and survive the fallout caused by the destruction of targets located upwind of the city. Over the decade after the Community Shelter Plan appeared in print, Spokane residents and others in the United States began to question the fundamental promise of survival offered by shelter plans, beginning around the time the food supplies in the shelters cruised past their expiration dates.

Shelters in Decline, 1970–1978

In Spokane, there are 251 aging fallout shelters, still stocked with food and supplies. They sit in rows of olive-drab metal cans: crackers, carbohydrate supplements, rudimentary medical supplies, sanitary supplies, and water.

—Dick Gentry

It was not an exaggeration when *Spokane Daily Chronicle* staff writer Dick Gentry described Spokane's public fallout shelters as "aging" in a December 18, 1976, article about the city's civil defense preparations. He could have used the word decrepit, as well. At the time of Gentry's article, Spokane's public shelters had been sitting in waiting since the early 1960s, and they were in need of resupplying. Years of neglect had left the shelter medicine and food stocks battered.[134]

The federally provided medical kits in United States public fallout shelters held phenobarbital sedative drug tablets that were attractive targets for thieves. In 1964, a person or persons had broken padlocks to steal drugs from a Washington State civil defense bunker located at Fort Casey. Other thefts certainly occurred in Washington State and across the United States that were possibly hushed-up by civil defense and law enforcement officials to avoid inspiring copy-cats. In 1966, the Department of Defense Office of Civil Defense sent a memo to all state and local civil defense directors in the United States, warning them to take precautions against drug thefts from public shelters. Despite the federal government's alert, pills continued to disappear. On October 1, 1971, Spokane Civil Defense Acting-Director Robert C. Pounds announced that robbers had stolen phenobarbital sedatives from approximately sixty public fallout shelters in Spokane County. In that same fall, the U.S. Office of Civil Defense ordered the removal of phenobarbital pills from the public fallout shelters in Spokane and Spokane County. Civil defense officials pulled 1.25 million sedative pills from 230 Spokane area fallout shelters. According to the *Spokane Daily Chronicle*, "Pounds and his aides mixed the pills and hot water into a 'slurry' and flushed the mixture into the sewage system."[135]

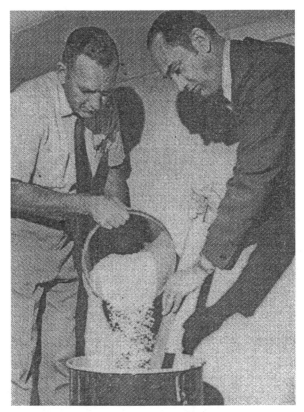

Figure 36   **Take that, you lousy dopers! In 1971, Spokane Acting-Director of Civil Defense Pounds and Spokane Deputy Director of Civil Defense Thomas R. Curtiss removed pills from the city's public shelters. (*Spokane Daily Chronicle*)**

Unlike the sedatives, the crackers in the shelters were not targeted by thieves. During the stocking phase of the fallout shelter program, the Department of Defense Office of Civil Defense had figured rightly that "the survival rations. . . should not be particularly tempting for peacetime use in competition with more normal food types." The problem with the crackers in the public shelters was that they were still on their shelves and no one was eating them.[136]

The crackers, which were not very palatable to begin with, became even less appetizing as they crept past their expiration dates. The Department of Defense had estimated in December 1961 that food supplies stocked in public shelters would have a shelf-life of five years. Since most United States public shelter stocking took place prior to 1965, most of the food supplies in shelters had reached their throw-away dates by 1970. In the fall of 1974, Seattle and Tacoma—in concert with seventeen other United States cities—pulled a total of 5 million tons of food from fallout shelters and shipped the provisions to people in need of food in Bangladesh, Africa, and South America. Spokane and Spokane County were not among the aid giving communities. On December 17, 1974, the *Spokane Daily Chronicle* let readers know that Spokane area shelter crackers would stay put. Emergency Services Acting-Director Robert C. Pounds said there was no money available for shipping the 493 tons of food supplies stocked in the city's shelters to a port. Spokane County Emergency Services Coordinator Ormel F. Ogden argued, "The fact is, the supplies are still good for the purposes they were put there for in the first place." Three years later, federal civil defense officials ordered local governments to destroy expired food supplies cached in public fallout shelters across the nation. A directive from the national agency advised that 100,000 tons of food supplies in America's shelters had "outlived their usefulness and no longer should be retained for human use." Washington State Emergency Services Director Betty McClelland asked her counterparts in local emergency services organizations to hold off on obeying the federal destruction order. Spokane Emergency Services Director Pounds and Spokane County Emergency Services Director Ogden followed McClelland's request and refused to get rid of the crackers. Ogden told reporters that most of the food in Spokane area fallout shelters was still edible. He acknowledged that some of the biscuits made of compressed wheat and cereal might be bad, but he claimed that the majority of the Spokane shelter food was made from baked biscuits that were still good to eat.[137]

The question of what to do with the survival rations was finally settled when the federal government abandoned the public fallout shelter system in 1978. As emergency services leaders in Spokane turned their attentions away from public shelter areas and adopted a different strategy for defending citizens against nuclear war, the building owners who had hosted the shelters were free to dispose of the crackers and other survival supplies however they pleased.

The End of the Public Shelter Program, 1978

The civil defense people make up the figures, not us.

—Jim Howard

Why did the public fallout shelter program last so long after the private fallout shelter fad ended in 1961? Political scientist Michael Lipsky speculates that part of the reason the public fallout shelter program did not collapse when support died for private shelters was that it required very little participation from the public. With a limited need for public approval (or backyard digging), the public shelter program—buoyed by its initial Congressional funding generated by Kennedy's Berlin Crisis speech in 1961, and heartened briefly by the flash of public shelter interest during the Cuban Missile Crisis in 1962—coasted through the 1960s and met Kennedy's goal to establish public shelters stocked with survival supplies in existing buildings. However, the program had problems maintaining its momentum. The factors that contributed to the demise of the private shelter fad—doubt that the shelters would actually stand up in the event of a nuclear war, concerns about the cost of shelters, troubling questions about the morality of shelters in society—also hampered the public fallout shelter program. In addition, there was an idea that shelters, if they actually worked, would endanger peace by conflicting with the policy of Mutually Assured Destruction (M.A.D.) that theorized neither the United States nor the Soviet Union would start a nuclear war as long as it meant both sides were guaranteed to perish in that war. Government and public interest in shelters also stayed low because the United States and the Soviet Union made moves toward detente by establishing a telephone hotline between the White House and the Kremlin for emergency communications on June 20, 1963, and signing a treaty banning atmospheric testing of nuclear weapons on August 5, 1963.[138]

Detente between the United States and the Soviet Union sapped support for the public shelter program—as did Vietnam. Historians Paul Boyer and Thomas J. Kerr have posited that the Vietnam War diverted the public's attention from civil defense. According to Kerr, "The civil defense question began to fade from public view by 1964, as the attention of the nation focused on the war in Vietnam." As Boyer put it, "The bomb was a potential menace; Vietnam was actuality." On June 29, 1965, Director Friend confirmed that the Vietnam War did not excite the same interest in civil defense among residents of Spokane as the Cuban Missile Crisis had. "We have had some increase in inquiries about procedures," he said, "but there is no comparison between the number of calls we are getting now and the number we received during the Cuban crisis of October 1962."[139]

The Vietnam War not only failed to interest the public in civil defense, but it also required federal money that otherwise may have been available to support fallout shelters. In February 1968, Secretary of Defense Robert S. McNamara told Congress that his 1969 defense budget plan reduced civil defense funding "to the lowest possible sustaining rate, pending the end of the Vietnam conflict." In 1970, John E. Davis, President Nixon's Director of the Office of Civil Defense, wrote, "Development of the U.S. civil defense system has been held at a minimum sustaining level, mainly because of (a) past reliance on 'massive retaliation' as our sole deterrent against attack, and (b) the high cost of our involvement in Vietnam."[140]

With civil defense a low priority, the federal government failed to take steps to replenish the food and medicine that deteriorated in public shelters. The government also did not advance the nation's public fallout shelter system beyond the limited plan inaugurated by Kennedy in 1961. Washington State Democratic Senator Henry M. Jackson, who had made his distaste for shelters known in 1961 when he chided America, "Don't get the idea that we can save ourselves from the Russian threat by digging a hole and crawling into it," helped scuttle a bill to fund additional public fallout shelters in March 1964. Not surprisingly, critics of the handling of the public shelter program had plenty to gripe about. In October 1971, the U.S. General Accounting Office informed Congress that "the nation lacks, and under current programs will continue to lack, a sufficient number of properly dispersed, adequately equipped fallout shelters in homes, schools, and other public buildings and facilities to accommodate the population in the event of a nuclear attack." Among the faults that the General Accounting Office identified in the ten-year-old public fallout shelter program, it highlighted the problem that the majority of the nation's shelters were located in "central urban areas" that were likely to be targeted and obliterated in the event of a Soviet nuclear attack.[141]

Critics of the state of the public fallout shelter program also hailed from Spokane. In February 1971, Kent Swigard of the *Spokesman-Review* wrote about three Spokane business managers who doubted the official estimates of how many people their buildings could shelter. Crescent Department Store Manager E. A. Pattison said that the Crescent could not hold the 7,690 people civil defense officials had designated it to accommodate. Pattison protested, "The civil defense people make up the figures, not us." Davenport Hotel General Manager Jim Howard was also skeptical about the role civil defense officials had cast for his building. "We're supposed to be able to take care of 4,600 people," Howard said, "but I don't know where we'd put them all." Civil defense planners estimated that the Ridpath Motor Inn and the Ridpath Hotel could together hold 7,169 people, but George A. Forbes, the general manager of both establishments, balked: "I don't see how we could ever take care of that many people." In contrast, there was at least one high-profile business manager who welcomed a crowd. Philip W. Alexander, the general manager of the downtown Bon Marche, proclaimed, "The Bon Marche is 10 stories high, covers three quarters of a city block and would be able to take care of its designated 17,998 people." Despite Alexander's testimony, there seemed to be good reason to believe that civil defense authorities had grossly over-estimated the capacities of Spokane's public shelters.[142]

Three days after Swigard's article threw Spokane's public shelter capabilities into doubt, the *Spokesman-Review* editorialized, "We have not mounted an effective organization to deal with nuclear attack. Let us either give up the illusion that we have done so, or put the organization to more useful work." The idea of taking a hard look at the worth of preparing a defense against nuclear war was seconded by a Spokane governmental watchdog group called the Little Hoover Commission. One of its members, Charles J. Tonani, announced on October 21, 1971, "the commission recommends the City Council review the civil defense operation and explore the possibility of channeling the funding into a more productive area."[143]

Criticism of Spokane area civil defense preparations culminated in 1972, when the Washington State legislature mandated that city and county governments in Washington State rechristen their civil defense groups as emergency services departments. Spokane city and county governments enthusiastically re-titled their civil defense departments and re-tasked them as well. Spokane Mayor David H. Rogers said on May 29, 1972, "The old Civil Defense procedures are out and we are reconstituting it as the Office of Emergency Services for just such things as earthquakes and floods." Spokane County also juggled titles and objectives. "Under the name Civil Defense," Spokane County Emergency Services Coordinator Ormel F. Ogden explained, "we were first concerned with nuclear disaster preparedness and let the rest follow but now we are emphasizing preparedness for natural disasters and, if that is in good shape, we'll be far down the road in being ready for nuclear disasters." It was a sure sign that civil defense preparations to survive nuclear war had lost importance with Spokane's movers and shakers when the planners of Expo '74—the international exposition that changed the face of Spokane's downtown river area—ignored a request from the federal Office of Civil Defense to include fallout shelters in the designs of buildings to be constructed on the exposition grounds.[144]

Shelters were falling out of favor with top leaders in the federal government as well. President Nixon considered replacing public shelters with an evacuation strategy, which had been the nation's primary civil defense plan when Nixon had served as Vice-President to President Eisenhower. President Ford commissioned studies of staging strategic retreats from cities in 1975. Finally, President Carter scrubbed shelters and implemented evacuation planning in September 1978. With President Carter's decision, the nation's nuclear war survival strategy changed from shelters back to evacuation.[145]

The White House policy shift impacted Spokane when federal civil defense officials and the Washington State Emergency Services Department helped Spokane authorities devise a Spokane area relocation plan in 1978 and 1979. The Spokane plan called for approximately 254,000 Spokane County residents to flee their homes and take refuge in communities in neighboring counties. Federal civil defense field officer Irving Silver said, "We figure in the relocation plan that there would be at least three people to a car, and that at a normal rate, the population of Spokane could leave the target area in eight hours."[146]

Since the federal government had resurrected an evacuation strategy, most of the public fallout shelters in the United States, including Spokane's, were unceremoniously decommissioned by building owners who swept out the civil defense survival supplies and reclaimed the abandoned shelter areas for their own storage purposes. Along with the clean sweep, many building owners also removed the metal signs that civil defense leaders had affixed to the outside walls of their buildings to advertise the shelters. The fallout shelter signs that survived often fell to vandals, souvenir hunters, and remodeling crews. Open season on the signs began in earnest in 1998 when the *Seattle Times* reported that the Washington State Department of Emergency Services was "encouraging cities and counties to remove those yellow-and-black signs." The call to take down the signs indicated that the public fallout shelter program was officially defunct and the shelters were irredeemable. The decommissioned public fallout shelters joined the backyard bunkers and basement hideaways as obsolete relics of the Cold War.[147]

Conclusion

After the Berlin Wall fell in 1989 and the Soviet Union collapsed in 1991, *Spokesman-Review* columnist Dan Hansen called Spokane's abandoned shelters "Cold War curiosities." In 1995, he followed his own curiosity to one of Spokane's backyard bunkers in the South Hill neighborhood. He found a shelter owned by a woman who did not wish to be named in print. She said she had never been a fan of the underground refuge and declared that it had been her husband's idea to build it. She tried to get rid of the bunker by donating it to the Cheney Cowles Museum (now the Northwest Museum of Arts and Culture), but the museum declined to dig it up. According to Hansen, the shelter was "too deteriorated for restoration."[148] While the state of the South Hill bunker made it unsuitable as a museum piece, the news of it served as a reminder that Spokane residents live among the relics of shelter mania. The Cold War is over, but the ruins of backyard bunkers, basement hideaways, and public fallout shelters exist as evidence of the fear of nuclear war that drove Spokane to take cover.

Bibliography

Primary Sources

Unpublished Primary Sources

Manuscripts

Balloch, John, James C. DeHaven, Bertrand Klass, John Mathewson, R. C. Raymond, Svend Riemer, Lawrence Livingston, Jr. "Spokane Civil Defense Exercise 'Operation Walkout'." 26 April 1954. National Academy of Sciences, Committee on Disaster Studies, Washington, D.C.

Civil Defense Scrapbooks, Spokane County Government, Emergency Management. Washington State Archives, Eastern Regional Branch, Cheney.

Horan, Walt, Papers. Manuscripts, Archives, and Special Collections, Washington State University, Pullman.

Jackson, Henry M., Papers. Special Collections Library, University of Washington, Seattle.

Magnuson, Warren, Papers. Special Collections Library, University of Washington, Seattle.

U.S. Corps of Engineers Walla Walla District Organization Plans and Publication Record Sets 1953–1970. Box 22, folder: 250/17, GEN (1961) Emergency Planning Files, Fallout Shelter Survey-COFF 31 Dec 61, FRT RHA Jun 63. National Archives-Pacific Alaska Region, Seattle.

Washington State Department of Civil Defense, Administration Subject Files. Accession 03-A-416. Washington State Archives, State Government Archives, Olympia.

Wesley S. Wagoner v. Audubon Fuel, Inc. Spokane Superior Court, case number 2-166293. Spokane County Clerk's Office Archives Department, Civil Roll No. 1973, document 1, 7.

Government

Federal

Glasstone, Samuel, ed. *The Effects of Nuclear Weapons.* Washington, D.C.: U.S. Government Printing Office, 1962.

U.S. Congress. Senate. Testimony of Dr. James E. McDonald at Hearings on Transportation Appropriations, March 2, 1971, Concerning the Supersonic Transport Program, 92d Cong., 1st sess. *Congressional Record* 117, pt. 6 (19 March 1971).

U.S. Department of Defense, Office of Civil Defense. *Fallout Protection: What to Know and Do About Nuclear Attack.* Washington, D.C.: U.S. Government Printing Office, 1961.

_____. *Instructions for Filling the Civil Defense Water-Storage Container.* Washington, D.C.: U.S. Government Printing Office, 1962.

_____. *Personal and Family Survival: Civil Defense Adult Education Course Student Manual.* Washington, D.C.: U.S. Government Printing Office, 1966.

_____. "Community Shelter Messages Go to 48 Million People." *Information Bulletin*, no. 245, 29 September 1970.

U.S. Department of Defense, Office of Civil Defense and Department of Health, Education, & Welfare Public Health Service. *Fallout Shelter Medical Kit Instructions*. July 1962. Author's collection.

U.S. Department of Energy, Assistant Secretary for Environmental, Safety, and Health. *Human Radiation Experiments: The Department of Energy Roadmap to the Story and the Records*. Oak Ridge: Office of Scientific and Technical Information, 1995.

U.S. Executive Office of the President, National Security Resources Board, Civil Defense Office. *Survival Under Atomic Attack*. Washington, D.C.: U.S. Government Printing Office, 1950.

U.S. Executive Office of the President, Office of Civil and Defense Mobilization. "Pittsburgh Study Concludes Two-Week Shelter Stay Shows No Serious Effects." *Information Bulletin*, no. 287, 14 March 1961.

U.S. Federal Civil Defense Administration. *Target Areas*. Washington, D.C.: U.S. Government Printing Office, 1951.

_____. *Target Areas for Civil Defense Purposes*. Washington, D.C.: U.S. Government Printing Office, 1953.

_____. *Facts About Fallout Protection*. Washington, D.C.: U.S. Government Printing Office, 1958.

U.S. General Accounting Office. *Activities and Status of Civil Defense in the United States: Report to the Congress by the Comptroller General of the United States*. Washington, D.C.: U.S. General Accounting Office, 1971.

U.S. Office of Civil and Defense Mobilization. *Fallout Shelter Surveys: Guide for Architects and Engineers*. Washington, D.C.: U.S. Government Printing Office, 1960.

_____. *Fallout Shelter Surveys: Guide for Executives*. Washington, D.C.: U.S. Government Printing Office, 1960.

State

State of Washington, Department of Civil Defense. *Civil Defense Bulletin*, no. 51, 21 March 1961.

_____. *Information Bulletin*, no. 85, 14 April 1954.

_____. *Information Bulletin*, no. 86, 30 April 1954.

_____. *Information Bulletin*, no. 115, 3 May 1956.

_____. *Information Bulletin*, no 163, April–May 1962.

_____. *Information Bulletin*, no 169, June July 1964.

Local

Spokane. "An ordinance changing the name of the Civil Defense Department of the City of Spokane to Emergency Services Department," Ordinance No. C21448 (1972).

Spokane City Plan Commission and U. S. Army Corps of Engineers. *Community Shelter Plan for Spokane and Spokane County*. Spokane: Spokane City and County Offices of Civil Defense, 1969.

Published Primary Sources

Books

Baker, George W., John H. Rohrer, and Mark J. Nearman. *Symposium on Human Problems in the Utilization of Fallout Shelters*. Washington, D.C.: National Academy of Sciences—National Research Council, 1960.

Kip, Lawrence. *Army Life on the Pacific; A Journal of the Expedition Against the Northern Indians, The Tribes of the Coeur D'Alenes, Spokans, and Pelouzes, in the Summer of 1858*. New York: Redfield, 1859.

Waskow, Arthur I., and Stanley L. Newman. *America in Hiding*. New York: Ballantine Books, 1962.

Magazines

"H-Bomb Odds: 1 Million to 1—And That's What May Save Us." *Newsweek*, 5 April 1954, 28.

"We Will Bury You!" *Time*, 26 November 1956, 24.

Newspapers

Fairchild Times (Wash.). 31 March; 21 April 1961.

Gonzagan (Spokane), Gonzagan Preparatory School, 25 March 1967.

Official Gazette of the City of Spokane, Washington 51, no. 42, 21 October 1961, 537.

Spokane Daily Chronicle. 9, 25 December 1941; 13, 14, 30 January; 3, 4, 22 June; 12 October; 30 November 1942; 26 March; 3

April; 10, 26 May; 16 November 1943; 17, 18, 21, 23 April
1952; 18, 19, 20, 23, 27, 28 March; 18 September; 22 October
1953; 23, 26 April 1954; 9 August; 25 December 1958; 19
February; 13 November 1959; 12, 29 March; 23, 24 May; 15,
25 August; 8 September; 8 October 1960; 2 June; 12, 13 July;
24 August; 13, 27 September; 2, 9, 13, 19, 24, 27, 30 October;
3, 7, 8, 9, 15, 19, 20, 29 November 1961; 5, 25 October 1962;
27 April; 7 May; 7 October; 5, 14 November 1963; 18
February; 20 August 1964; 29 June 1965; 2 January; 1, 3, 18
February; 11, 13, 15 March; 3 April; 16, 24 July; 20 November
1967; 16 February; 6 April; 31 October; 28 November 1968; 6,
12 November 1969; 1, 21 October 1971; 18 September 1973;
17 December 1974; 18 December 1976; 8 January 1977; 7
March 1978; 17 January 1979.

Spokesman-Review (Spokane). 7, 9, 11 December 1941; 10 March;
27 April; 5, 9 December 1942; 19 January; 26 March; 13 July;
2 October 1943; 8, 15, 16 August 1945; 8, 9 December 1950; 3
March 1951; 15 October 1953; 24, 26, 27, 28 April; 27 May
1954; 19 March 1955; 9 July 1957; 29 March; 25 May; 10
August; 16 October 1960; 5 March; 1 May; 2 June; 27 July; 30
August; 1, 3, 26, 28 September; 8, 19, 22 October; 9, 10, 11,
12, 13, 18, 19, 26 November; 2, 14, 16 December 1961; 6
May; 8 July; 24, 26, 28 October 1962; 27 June 1963; 25 March
1964; 7 January; 18 February 1965; 13 May 1966; 13 March;
22 October; 20 December 1967; 11 November 1968; 1, 7, 21
November 1969; 14, 17 February, 6 October 1971, 30 May
1973; 4 February 1977; 5 December 1978; 28 April 1995; 25
July 1999; 6 May 2001; 21 March 2003; 29 September 2005;
21 September 2007.

Secondary Sources

Books

Bamonte, Tony, and Suzanne Schaefer Bamonte. *Miss Spokane: Elegant Ambassadors and Their City.* Spokane: Tornado Creek Publications, 2000.

Blanchard, B. Wayne. *American Civil Defense 1945–1984: The Evolution Of Programs and Policies.* Washington, D.C.: U.S. Government Printing Office, 1989.

Boutwell, Florence Otto. *The Spokane Valley, Volume 4: The Naval Supply Depot at Velox.* Spokane: Arthur Clark Company, 2004.

Boyer, Paul. *By the Bomb's Early Light: American Thought and Culture at the Dawn of the Atomic Age.* New York: Panthenon, 1985. Reprint, Chapel Hill: University of North Carolina Press, 1994.

Brown, Joseph C., ed. *The Rainbow Seekers: Stories of Spokane, the Expo City, and the Inland Empire.* Spokane: Wescoast Publishing, 1974.

Chang, Laurence, and Peter Kornbluh, eds. *The Cuban Missile Crisis, 1962: A National Security Archive Documents Reader.* New York: New Press, 1992.

Chivian, Eric, Susanna Chivian, Robert Jay Lifton, John E. Mack, eds., *Last Aid: The Medical Dimensions of Nuclear War.* San Francisco: W. H. Freeman and Company, 1982.

D'Antonio, Michael. *Atomic Harvest: Hanford and the Lethal Toll of America's Nuclear Arsenal.* New York: Crown, 1993.

Fahey, John. *Saving the Reservation: Joe Garry and the Battle to Be Indian.* Seattle: University of Washington Press, 2001.

Gerber, Michele Stenehjem. *On the Home Front: The Cold War Legacy of the Hanford Nuclear Site*, 3rd ed. Lincoln: University of Nebraska Press, 2007.

Granick, Harry. *Underneath New York*. New York: Rinehart & Company, 1947.

Grossman, Andrew D. *Neither Dead Nor Red: Civilian Defense and American Political Development During the Early Cold War*. New York: Routledge, 2001.

Henriksen, Margot A. *Dr. Strangelove's America: Society and Culture in the Atomic Age*. Berkeley: University of California Press, 1997.

Judge, Edward H., and John W. Langdon. *The Cold War: A History Through Documents*. Upper Saddle River, New Jersey: Prentice Hall, 1999.

Kardong, Don. *Bloomsday: A City in Motion*. Spokane: Cowles Publishing Company, 1989.

Kaufman, Robert G. *Henry M. Jackson: A Life in Politics*. Seattle: University of Washington Press, 2000.

Kerr, Thomas J. *Civil Defense in the U. S.: Bandaid for a Holocaust?* Boulder, Colo: Westview Press, 1983.

Kershner, Jim. *Carl Maxey: A Fighting Life*. Seattle: University of Washington Press, 2008.

Kip, Lawrence. *Indian War in the Pacific Northwest: The Journal of Lieutenant Lawrence Kip*. With an introduction by Clifford E. Trafzer. Lincoln: University of Nebraska Press, 1999.

Lanford, Jill M. "The World War II Home Front in Spokane: A Changing World, A Changing Community." Master's thesis, Eastern Washington University, 1966.

Leaning, Jennifer, and Langley Keyes. *The Counterfeit Ark: Crisis Relocation for Nuclear War.* Cambridge, Mass.: Ballinger Publishing, 1984.

Lonnquest, John C., and David F. Winkler. *To Defend and Deter: The Legacy of the United States Cold War Missile Program.* Washington, D. C.: U. S. Government Printing Office, 1997.

MacGregor, Wayne C. *Through These Portals: A Pacific War Saga.* Pullman, Wash.: Washington State University Press, 2002.

May, Ernest R., and Phillip D. Zelikow, eds. *The Kennedy Tapes: Inside the White House During the Cuban Missile Crisis.* Cambridge, Mass.: The Belknap Press of Harvard University Press, 1998.

McCash, William. *Bombs Over Brookings: The World War II Bombings of Curry County, Oregon and the Postwar Friendship Between Brookings and the Japanese Pilot, Nobuo Fujita.* Bend, Ore.: Maverick Publications, 2005.

McEnaney, Laura. *Civil Defense Begins at Home: Militarization Meets Everyday Life in the Fifties.* Princeton: Princeton University Press, 2000.

Meyer, Bette E. *Fort George Wright: Not Only Where the Band Played.* Fairfield, Wash.: Ye Galleon Press, 1994.

Mikesh, Robert C. *Japan's World War II Balloon Bomb Attacks on North America.* Washington, D. C.: Smithsonian Institution Press, 1973.

Morgan, Mark L., and Mark A. Berhow. *Rings of Supersonic Steel: Air Defenses of the United States Army 1950–1979, An Introductory History and Site Guide*, 2d ed. Bodega Bay, Calif.: Fort MacArthur Military Press, 2002.

Morrissey, Katherine G. *Mental Territories: Mapping the Inland Empire*. Ithaca: Cornell University Press, 1997.

Nicholson, Graham. *Surviving the Blitz: Stockport Air Raid Shelters, 1939–1945*. Stockport: Stockport Metropolitan Borough Museum and Art Gallery Service, 1990.

Noran, Edward W. *"A Night of Terror, Devastation, Suffering and Awful Woe.": The Spokane Fire of 1889*. Spokane: Eastern Washington State Historical Society, 1989.

Nunemaker, Carolyn Hage. *Downtown Spokane Images, 1930–1949*. Spokane: National Color Graphics, 1997.

O'L. Higgins, Shaun, and Laura B. Lee, eds. *Ice Storm '96: Days of Darkness, Days of Cold: A Pictorial Record of the Worst Winter Storm in the History of the Inland Northwest*. Spokane: New Media Ventures, 1996.

Oakes, Guy. *The Imaginary War: Civil Defense and the American Cold War Culture*. New York: Oxford University Press, 1994.

Office of the Wing Historian, 92d Air Refueling Wing. *A Brief History of Fairchild AFB, Washington and the 92d Air Refueling Wing*. Fairchild AFB, Wash.: Office of the Wing Historian, 92d Air Refueling Wing, 2006.

Peterson, Jeannie, ed. *Aftermath: The Human and Ecological Consequences of Nuclear War*. New York: Pantheon, 1983.

Pieroth, Doris H., *The Hutton Settlement: A Home for One Man's Family*. Spokane: The Hutton Settlement, 2003.

Podvig, Pavel, ed. *Russian Strategic Nuclear Forces*. Cambridge: The MIT Press, 2001.

Rose, Kenneth D. *One Nation Underground: The Fallout Shelter in American Culture*. New York: New York University Press, 2001.

Rourke, Norman Edward. *War Comes to Alaska: The Dutch Harbor Attack June 3–4, 1942*. Shippensburg: Burd Street Press, 1997.

Scates, Shelby. *Warren G. Magnuson and the Shaping of Twentieth-Century America*. Seattle: University of Washington Press, 1998.

Schlicke, Carl P. *General George Wright: Guardian of the Pacific Coast*. Norman, Okla.: University of Oklahoma Press, 1988.

Shore, Marshall B. *War Stories: True Stories of World War II and the Cold War as Experienced by the Author during over Thirty Years Serving in the United States Army Air Corps, the Air Reserve, the Air National Guard and as an Officer in the United States Air Force*. Spokane: Arthur H. Clark, 2000.

Virilio, Paul. *Bunker Archeology*. New York: Princeton Architectural Press, 1994.

Wang, David, ed. *Sounding Spokane: Perspectives on the Built Environment of a Regional City*. Spokane: Eastern Washington University Press, 2003.

Wigner, Eugene P. *Who Speaks for Civil Defense?* New York: Charles Scribner's Sons, 1968.

Winkler, Allan M. *Life Under A Cloud*. New York: Oxford University Press, 1993.

Wordie, Jason and Ko Tim Keung. *Ruins of War: A Guide to Hong Kong's Battlefields and Wartime Sites*. Hong Kong: Joint Publishing, 1996.

done
Lee O'Connor

Youngs, J. William T. *The Fair and the Falls: Spokane's Expo '74: Transforming an American Environment*. Cheney, Wash.: Eastern Washington University Press, 1996.

Scholarly Articles

Burns, Robert Ignatius, S.J. "Pere Joset's Account of the Indian War of 1858." *Pacific Northwest Quarterly* 38, no. 4 (October 1947): 285–314.

Denfeld, Duane Colt. "ICBM (Intercontinental Ballistic Missiles) in Washington State." *History Link* (July 2012). http://www.historylink.org/index.cfm?DisplayPage=output.cfm&file_id=10158 [accessed December 5, 2013].

Johnson, Randall A. "The Ordeal of the Steptoe Command." *The Pacific Northwesterner* 17, no. 9 (Winter 1973). http://www.historylink.org/index.cfm?DisplayPage=output.cfm&file_id=8123 [accessed January 15, 2009].

Karp, Walter. "When Bunkers Last in the Backyard Bloom'd." *American Heritage* 31, no. 2 (February/March 1980): 84–93.

Kershner, Jim. "Segregation in Spokane: Longtime Black Residents Recount the Injustices and the Victories." *Columbia: The Magazine of Northwest History* 14, no. 4 (Winter 2000–1): 38–44.

138

Notes

Introduction

1 Pia K. Hansen, "How Many Huge Holes Are in Back Yards Across Spokane?" *Spokesman-Review*, 29 September 2005, Z3.

I. Shelter Mania

2 Kent Graybill, "Tales of a Shopping Bag," *Southside Shopper*, Spokane, 18 July 1962. This article, with no page information, is located in Civil Defense Scrapbooks, Spokane County Government, Emergency Management, Accession #997-0389. Washington State Archives, Eastern Regional Branch, Cheney. Hereafter referred to as Civil Defense Scrapbooks, WSA, ERB, Cheney; Nikita Khrushchev, quoted in "We Will Bury You!" *Time*, 26 November 1956, 24; and June G. Potter, letter to the editor, *Spokesman-Review*, 12 November 1961, 4.

3 Arthur I. Waskow and Stanley L. Newman, *America in Hiding* (New York: Ballantine Books, 1962), 9; Historian Kenneth D. Rose called Kennedy's speech the "flashpoint" of the shelter phenomenon. Kenneth D. Rose, *One Nation Underground: The Fallout Shelter in American Culture* (New York: New York University Press, 2001), 2, 79–80; and John F. Kennedy, "Radio and Television Report to the American People," 25 July 1961. An audio recording of the speech and a transcript of Kennedy's words are available online from the John F. Kennedy Presidential Library and Museum, http://www.jfklibrary.org/Historical+Resources/Archives/Reference+Des k/Speeches/JFK/003POF03BerlinCrisis07251961.htm (accessed March 23, 2009).

4 Kennedy delivered his moon speech in a "Special Message to the Congress on National Urgent Needs," 25 May 1961. An excerpt of an audio recording of the speech and a transcript are available from the John F. Kennedy Presidential Library and Museum, http://www.jfklibrary.org/Historical+Resources/Archives/Reference+Des k/Speeches/JFK/003POF03NationalNeeds05251961.htm (accessed March 23, 2009).

5 "Teachers Called Pupil Guarders," *Spokesman-Review*, 8 December 1950, 6; Federal Civil Defense Administration, *Target Areas* (Washington, D.C.: U.S. Government Printing Office, 1951), 12; Federal Civil Defense Administration, *Advisory Bulletin*, no. 149, 14 September 1953, 1; Federal Civil Defense Administration, *Target Areas for Civil Defense Purposes* (Washington, D.C.: U.S. Government Printing Office, 1953). The FCDA documents are collected in Washington State Civil Defense, Administration Subject Files, Accession 03-A-416, box 10, folder: Target Areas 1951–65, Washington State Archives, State Government Archives, Olympia. Hereafter referred to as Civil Defense Files, 03-A-416, WSA, SGA, Olympia; and "Spokane Area Rated High on Russian Bombing List," *Spokane Daily Chronicle*, 18 September 1953, 3.

6 Spokane's post-war boom is analyzed in David Wang and Douglas Williams Menzies, "Brown's Addition: A Mirror of Spokane," in *Sounding Spokane: Perspectives on the Built Environment of a Regional City*, ed. David Wang (Spokane: Eastern Washington University Press, 2003), 18; Office of the Wing Historian, 92d Air Refueling Wing, *A Brief History of Fairchild AFB, Washington and the 92d Air Refueling Wing* (Fairchild AFB, Wash.: Office of the Wing Historian, 92d Air Refueling Wing, 2006), 5, 6, 14; Jim Camden, "No More Nukes at Fairchild: Spokane's Nuclear Era Went Out, Not With A Bang Thankfully," *Spokesman-Review*, 6 May 2001; Fairchild AFB was originally the Spokane Army Air Depot, which was established on

March 1, 1942. During WWII, the base was nicknamed the "Galena Army Air Depot." In October 1944, the Spokane Army Air Depot became the Spokane Air Depot. In 1947 it was called the Spokane Army Air Field. In 1948, the site was renamed the Spokane Air Force Base. In 1950, the name changed to Fairchild Air Force Base. John L. Poole, "A Historical Account of the Socio-Economic Relationship Between Fairchild Air Force Base and Spokane, Washington" (master's thesis, Eastern Washington University, 1976), 44–45, 54–55, 61, 68; John C. Lonnquest and David F. Winkler, *To Defend and Deter: The Legacy of the United States Cold War Missile Program* (Washington, D.C.: U.S. Government Printing Office, 1997), 561–562; For maps and photographs of the missiles and bases see Silo World, http://www.siloworld.com (accessed November 30, 2008); Tony Bamonte and Suzanne Schaefer Bamonte, *Miss Spokane: Elegant Ambassadors and Their City* (Spokane: Tornado Creek Publications, 2000), 90, 215–216, 225; "Col. Jeffrey Ceremony Speaker at Christening of 'Inland Empire' Missile," *Fairchild Times*, 31 March 1961, 1; and Gottfried S. Ehrenberg, letter to the editor, *Spokesman-Review*, 6 May 1958, 4.

7 Rose, *One Nation Underground*, 166; and Lonnquest and Winkler, *To Defend and Deter*, 69–70.

8 "Defense Called Job of Everyone," *Spokesman-Review*, 15 October 1953, 6; and George Cheek, "If Spokane Were Bombed [Part One]," *Spokesman-Review*, 9 July 1957, 1.

9 Pavel Podvig, ed., *Russian Strategic Nuclear Forces* (Cambridge: The MIT Press, 2001), 5, 123.

10 Gallup Poll 1960, 3:1654 as cited in W. J. Rorabaugh, *Kennedy and the Promise of the Sixties* (Cambridge, England: Cambridge University Press, 2002), 37; and Associated Press, "Spokane Talk by

Kennedy Raps Defense," *Moses Lake (Wash.) Columbia Basin Daily Herald,* 12 February 1960, 5.

11 Joseph H. Boyd to Mrs. Boyd, 11 August 1889, as cited in Edward W. Noran, *"A Night of Terror, Devastation, Suffering and Awful Woe.": The Spokane Fire of 1889* (Spokane: Eastern Washington State Historical Society, 1989), 37; "A-Bomb Killing Potential Is Figured at 8,000 Lives," *Spokane Daily Chronicle,* 26 April 1954, 3; and "Civil Defenders Advised to Plan," *Spokesman-Review,* 19 March 1955, 1.

12 The Soviet super bomb of 1961 still holds this dubious honor. Frighteningly, the Soviets had dialed down the weapon's blast size. It had a potential yield of 100-megatons. Podvig, ed., *Russian Strategic Nuclear Forces,* 450, 444–445; "No 'Bomb' Terror Seen," *Spokane Daily Chronicle,* 31 October 1961, 3; "If 'It' Hit Here: 14 Mile Area of Death Seen by Defense Chief," *Spokane Daily Chronicle,* 30 October 1961, 1; Some of the other zones of complete destruction in Washington included Seattle, Tacoma, Olympia, Hanford, and Grand Coulee Dam. A copy of the target map was attached to a letter that the Washington State Civil Defense Director sent to a Denver resident. Charles C. Ralls to Walter Posner, 15 March 1962, Civil Defense Files, 03-A-416, box 10, Folder: Target Areas 1951–65, WSA, SGA, Olympia.

13 Kent Graybill, "Tales of a Shopping Bag," *Southside Shopper,* Spokane, 18 July 1962. Civil Defense Scrapbooks, WSA, ERB, Cheney; City of Spokane Fire Department Deputy-Chief A. L. O'Connor warned the city in 1971 that a nuclear bomb set off near Spokane could ignite a rash of fires in the city that could coalesce into the type of firestorm that devastated German and Japanese cities that fell under Allied bombing attacks during World War II. According to Deputy-Chief O'Connor, if a firestorm hit Spokane, "There would be no way the Fire Department could stop it from burning the entire city." Kent Swigard, "Civil Defense Fights Apathy," 1; Eric Chivian and othes, eds., *Last Aid: The Medical Dimensions of Nuclear War* (San Francisco: W. H.

Freeman and Company, 1982; Jeannie Peterson, ed., *Aftermath: The Human and Ecological Consequences of Nuclear War* (New York: Pantheon, 1983); For the story of the crew aboard a Japanese fishing vessel called the *Lucky Dragon*, who suffered from an accidental exposure to fallout from a United States bomb test in the Pacific in 1954, see Allan M. Winkler, *Life Under A Cloud* (New York: Oxford University Press, 1993), 93–94.

14 Federal Civil Defense Administration, *Facts About Fallout Protection* (Washington, D.C.: U.S. Government Printing Office, 1958); and U.S. Office of Civil and Defense Mobilization, *Fallout Shelter Surveys: Guide for Executives* (Washington, D.C.: U.S. Government Printing Office, 1960), 1–2.

15 U.S. Office of Civil and Defense Mobilization, *Fallout Shelter Surveys: Guide for Architects and Engineers* (Washington, D.C.: U.S. Government Printing Office, 1960), 3.

16 "Defense Shelters Found for 382,900," *Spokane Daily Chronicle*, 5 October 1962, 3; U.S. Office of Civil and Defense Mobilization, *Fallout Shelter Surveys: Guide for Architects and Engineers*, 3; and Thomas J. Kerr, *Civil Defense in the U.S.: Bandaid for a Holocaust?* (Boulder, Colo.: Westview Press, 1983), 116, 129–130.

17 Unfortunately, fallout was not a hazard that was limited to nuclear war. The U.S. government declassified documents in 1986 that detailed accidental and intentional releases of radiation from the Hanford Atomic Bomb Works in the 1940s and 1950s. Spokane was downwind of emissions from Hanford and it was also subject to fallout that traveled the globe as a result of atmospheric testing of nuclear weapons. Michele Stenehjem Gerber, *On the Home Front: The Cold War Legacy of the Hanford Nuclear Site*, 3rd ed. (Lincoln: University of Nebraska Press, 2007), 76, 79, 90–92, 201; Michael D'Antonio, *Atomic Harvest: Hanford*

and the *Lethal Toll of America's Nuclear Arsenal* (New York: Crown, 1993), 2, 90; Karen Dorn Steele, "Fallout Studies Incomplete, Scientists Says Releases From Weapons Tests Must Be Added To Hanford Doses For Accuracy, He Argues," *Spokesman-Review*, 25 July 1999, B1; Jack Roberts, "Data on Survival Being Dusted Off," *Spokesman-Review*, 28 October 1962, 8; "High Survival Rate Seen," *Spokane Daily Chronicle*, 14 November 1963, 5; and Jack Roberts, "Residents Are Urged to Install Shelters," *Spokesman-Review*, 3 September 1961, 1.

18 Gerber, *On the Home Front*, 102; and Department of Civil Defense, State of Washington, *Information Bulletin*, no. 115, 3 May 1956, 1, Civil Defense Files, 03-A-416, box 21, folder: Civil Defense Bulletins (Information Bulletins) 1956–1957, WSA, SGA, Olympia.

19 McDonald's letter and Jackson's scenario appeared in "Senator, Defense Officials Deny Missiles Swell Peril," *Spokane Daily Chronicle*, 13 November 1959, 7; McDonald was one of the earliest scientists to urge stewardship of the Earth's ozone layer to prevent an increase in the number of skin cancers caused by ultra-violet radiation. In 1971, he testified before Congress against the development of supersonic transport planes because of the harm they could do to the ozone layer. Congress, Senate, Testimony of Dr. James E. McDonald at Hearings on Transportation Appropriations, March 2, 1971, Concerning the Supersonic Transport Program, 92d Cong., 1st sess., *Congressional Record* 117, pt. 6 (19 March 1971): 7252–7256; However, McDonald is best known for alleging that the Air Force's Project Bluebook failed to make a good-faith effort to scientifically investigate the U.F.O. phenomenon. James E. McDonald, "Science in Default: Twenty-two Years of Inadequate UFO Investigations," in *UFO's: A Scientific Debate*, ed. Carl Sagan and Thornton Page (Ithaca: Cornell University Press, 1972), 52; *The Spokesman-Review* boosted the Atlas missile bases in "Spokane Seen as Likely Site for Giant New Multi-Million Dollar ICBM Base," *Spokesman-Review*, 5 April 1958, 1; Editorial, "Missile Base Here

Would Be Welcomed," *Spokesman-Review*, 5 April 1958, 4; editorial cartoon, "Intercontinental Ballistic Mi$$ile," *Spokesman-Review*, 8 April 1958, 4. For Sen. Jackson as "the congressional representative for the military-industrial complex," see Robert G. Kaufman, *Henry M. Jackson: A Life in Politics* (Seattle: University of Washington Press, 2000), 177; Jackson was also known as "the Senator from Boeing." Shelby Scates, *Warren G. Magnuson and the Shaping of Twentieth-Century America* (Seattle: University of Washington Press, 1998), 126.

20 John F. Kennedy, "Radio and Television Report to the American People," 25 July 1961. An audio recording of the speech and a transcript of Kennedy's words are available online from the John F. Kennedy Presidential Library and Museum, http://www.jfklibrary.org/Historical+Resources/Archives/Reference+Desk/Speeches/JFK/003POF03BerlinCrisis07251961.htm (accessed March 23, 2009); "If 'It' Hit Here: 14 Mile Area of Death Seen by Defense Chief," *Spokane Daily Chronicle*, 30 October 1961, 1; and Kelso, "Addresses Survival Meet Here," 10.

21 "Need Seen for Fallout Shelters," *Spokane Daily Chronicle*, 2 January 1967, 25; Spokane City Plan Commission and U.S. Army Corps of Engineers, *Community Shelter Plan for Spokane and Spokane County* (Spokane: City and County Offices of Civil Defense, 1969); and Kent Swigard, "Civil Defense Fights Apathy," *Spokesman-Review*, 14 February 1971, 1.

II. Shelters in the Indian Wars, 1858, 1877

22 "Idaho Welcome," *Fairchild Times* (Wash.), 21 April 1961, 1; Wright's description of his route appears in Carl P. Schlicke, *General George Wright: Guardian of the Pacific Coast* (Norman, Okla.: University of Oklahoma Press, 1988), 178; Joseph Garry's accomplishments included his military services in WWII and the Korean War, his long

tenure as a chairman and member of the Coeur d' Alene Tribal Council, his presidency of the National Congress of American Indians from 1953 to 1959, his successful fight to prevent the U.S. Congress from terminating Indian reservations and dissolving tribes, and his election to the Idaho senate. John Fahey, *Saving the Reservation: Joe Garry and the Battle to Be Indian* (Seattle: University of Washington Press, 2001), 103, 107; and Fahey, "Garry, Joseph," in *Encyclopedia of North American Indians*, 1996 ed., 215–216.

23 Fort George Wright was established in Spokane at the end of the nineteenth century. Infantry troops were trained at the fort from 1899 to 1940. In 1941, the Army Air Force took over Fort George Wright. In 1946, Fort George Wright became home to the 15th Air Force. In 1949, Fort George Wright was renamed George Wright Air Force Base. In 1957, the base was shut down and declared surplus. Bette E. Meyer, *Fort George Wright: Not Only Where the Band Played* (Fairfield, Wash.: Ye Galleon Press, 1994), 32, 79–80, 84; "Col. Jeffrey Ceremony Speaker at Christening of 'Inland Empire' Missile," *Fairchild Times*, 31 March 1961, 1; Two years later, another Miss Spokane winner, Natalie Monte, performed the same rite for a B-52 nuclear bomber called the *City of Spokane*. Bamonte and Schaefer Bamonte, *Miss Spokane*, 90, 215–216, 225.

24 Schlicke, *General George Wright*, 141–143, 145–147; Lawrence Kip, *Army Life on the Pacific; A Journal of the Expedition Against the Northern Indians, The Tribes of the Coeur D' Alenes, Spokans, and Pelouzes, in the Summer of 1858* (New York: Redfield, 1859), 12; Randall A. Johnson, "The Ordeal of the Steptoe Command," *Pacific Northwester* 17, no. 9 (Winter 1973) http://www.historylink.org/index.cfm?DisplayPage=output.cfm&file_id=8123 (accessed March 25, 2009); For a list of Indian weapons used against Steptoe's force see Schlicke, *General George Wright*, 147.

25 Ibid., 142–143, 158, 166–167, 170–172.

26 Ibid., 176–178, 184; Wright, as quoted by Kip, *Army Life*, 67–68.

27 Joseph C. Brown, ed., *The Rainbow Seekers: Stories of Spokane, the Expo City, and the Inland Empire* (Spokane: Wescoast Publishing, 1974), 54; Robert Ignatius Burns, S.J., "Pere Joset's Account of the Indian War of 1858," *Pacific Northwest Quarterly* 38, no. 4 (October 1947): 285; Trafzer, introduction to Kip, *Indian War*, xvi; and Katherine G. Morrissey, *Mental Territories: Mapping the Inland Empire* (Ithaca: Cornell University Press, 1997), 60.

28 J. William T. Youngs, *The Fair and the Falls: Spokane's Expo '74: Transforming An American Environment* (Cheney: Eastern Washington University Press, 1996), 25–26.

III. World War II Shelters, 1941–1945

29 "Defense Effort Given Approval: Poll Shows Spokane Citizens Do Not Fear Bombs." This clipping, with no publishing information provided other than "June '42," is in Civil Defense Scrapbooks, WSA, ERB, Cheney; After the initial battles in Dutch Harbor, American and Japanese forces skirmished in Alaska's Aleutian Island chain off-and-on until the Japanese retreated in July 1943. Norman Edward Rourke, *War Comes to Alaska: The Dutch Harbor Attack, June 3–4, 1942* (Shippensburg: Burd Street Press, 1997), 4, 39–40, 47, 59, 89–90; "Alaska Is Bombed By the Japanese," *Spokane Daily Chronicle*, 3 June 1942, 1; "Dutch Harbor Brings Attack Close to Home," *Spokane Daily Chronicle*, 4 June 1942, 3; "Axis Sub Shells Oregon Fort Area," *Spokane Daily Chronicle*, 22 June 1942, 1; The Japanese attacked Oregon a second and third time in September 1942, but the events went unreported in Spokane. On September 9, 1942, a Japanese pilot named Nobuo Fujita launched his plane from the deck of a Japanese submarine floating off the coast of

Oregon and dropped two 170-pound incendiary bombs near Brookings, Oregon. Fujita dropped two more incendiary bombs on September 29, 1942. The Japanese hoped that Fujita would succeed in setting Oregon's forested coastal area ablaze. The September 9 attack did cause a small fire, but it was easily extinguished by the U.S. Forest Service. The second attack, on September 29, 1942, did not succeed in starting any fires. William McCash, *Bombs Over Brookings: The World War II Bombings of Curry County, Oregon and the Postwar Friendship Between Brookings and the Japanese Pilot, Nobuo Fujita* (Bend, Ore.: Maverick Publications, 2005), 1, 7, 17, 43.

30 "Brings Warning to Home Front," *Spokesman-Review*, 13 July 1943, 7; "Jap Bomb Hit Near Hanford," *Spokesman-Review*, 16 August 1945, 3; Robert C. Mikesh warned in 1973 that "hundreds of these balloons were never found and may still be detonated with the slightest contact." Robert C. Mikesh, *Japan's World War II Balloon Bomb Attacks on North America* (Washington, D.C.: Smithsonian Institution Press, 1973), 1, 21, 25–27, 38, 71, 82.

31 Jill M. Lanford, "The World War II Home Front in Spokane: A Changing World, A Changing Community" (master's thesis, Eastern Washington University, 1966), 6, 33; Anonymous, *Spokane and the Inland Empire: Frontier of the New Industrial West* (Spokane: 1945), 31; Marshall B. Shore, *War Stories: True Stories of World War II and the Cold War as Experienced by the Author During over Thirty Years Serving in the United States Army Air Corps, the Air Reserve, the Air National Guard and as an Officer in the United States Air Force* (Spokane: Arthur H. Clark: 2000), 136; John L. Poole, "A Historical Account of the Socio-Economic Relationship Between Fairchild Air Force Base and Spokane, Washington" (master's thesis, Eastern Washington University, 1976), 44–45, 54–55; Meyer, *Fort George Wright*, 28–29, 79; and Florence Otto Boutwell, *The Spokane Valley, Volume 4: The Naval Supply Depot at Velox* (Spokane: Arthur Clark Company, 2004), 15, 19, 37, 43.

32 "Radios Silenced, Coast Darkened," *Spokesman-Review*, 9
December 1941, 1; and "Prepare for Blackout Spokane Is Warned,"
Spokane Daily Chronicle, 9 December 1941, 1.

33 Advertisement, *Spokane Daily Chronicle*, 30 January 1942, 14;
"Use of Adhesive on Windows Hit," *Spokane Daily Chronicle*, 25
December 1941, 3; and Carolyn Hage Nunemaker, *Downtown Spokane
Images, 1930–1949* (Spokane: National Color Graphics, 1997), 151.

34 "Radios Silenced, Coast Darkened," 1; "Prepare for Blackout
Spokane," 1; "Blackout Plans for Region Told," *Spokesman-Review*, 11
December 1941, 6; The federal government didn't order people of
Japanese ancestry living in Spokane to go to internment camps but two
Japanese community leaders were arrested and then detained at a
government internment camp, where they were interrogated. The City of
Spokane enforced a curfew for the Japanese and refused to issue business
licenses to Japanese people during the war. Nonetheless, historian
Deborah Ann Gallacci Wilbert asserts that Spokane Japanese were
shielded from extreme forms of government discrimination by business
partners and allies in the white community. Deborah Ann Gallacci
Wilbert, "A History of the Formation of the Japanese American
Community in Spokane, Washington, 1890–1941" (master's thesis,
Washington State University, 1982), 104–112.

35 "City Is Proud of Its Blackout," *Spokesman-Review*, 9 December
1942, 6; "Spokane Is Ready, Blackout Shows," *Spokesman-Review*, 26
March 1943, 1; "City Blackout Is Successful," *Spokesman-Review*, 2
October 1943, 6; and "Drill in Memory of Pearl Harbor," *Spokane Daily
Chronicle*, 30 November 1942, 3.

36 Wayne C. MacGregor, *Through These Portals: A Pacific War Saga*
(Pullman: Washington State University Press, 2002), 35, 51; John J.
Lemon, "Blackout Drill Results Called Most Effective," *Spokane Daily
Chronicle*, 26 March 1943, 5; "Desire for Light Brings His Arrest,"

Spokane Daily Chronicle, 26 March 1943, 1; and "City Blackout Is Successful," 6.

37 "'Forget It,' Defense Chief Tells Raid Shelter Planner," *Spokane Daily Chronicle*, 13 January 1942, 3.

38 "Owners of Buildings Here Take Air Raid Precautions," *Spokane Daily Chronicle*, 14 January 1942, 6; and "One of First Spokane Homes with Shelter Against Raids," *Spokane Daily Chronicle*, 14 January 1942, 5.

39 "Downtown Air Raid Shelter Wins City O.K.," *Spokesman-Review*, 10 March 1942, 6; "Downtown Air Raid Shelter Available Soon," *Spokane Daily Chronicle*, 27 April 1942, 5; and Betta Ferrendelli, "Four Generations of Cowles Build Diverse Empire," *Puget Sound Business Journal* (Seattle), 9 November 2001, http://seattle.bizjournals.com/seattle/stories/2001/11/12/focus3.html (accessed March 24, 2009).

40 "Plans Ready for Blackout Test Monday," *Spokane Daily Chronicle*, 5 December 1942, 6; "Select 20 Air Raid Shelters," *Spokesman-Review*, 19 January 1943, 1; Spokane City Plan Commission and U.S. Army Corps of Engineers, *Community Shelter Plan*; Lemon, "Blackout Drill Results," 5; Spokane City Plan Commission and U.S. Army Corps of Engineers, *Community Shelter Plan*; and "Jinnett Is Heading Shelter Committee," *Spokane Daily Chronicle*, 26 May 1943, 7.

41 Mrs. Fred B. Huerlin, "Block Mothers Here Prepared for Emergency," *Spokane Daily Chronicle*, 12 October 1942, 3.

42 Arthur J. Freeborg, "Letter to the Editor: Rates Civilian Defense Set-Up As Of No Avail," a handwritten notation on the article says "R 3/6," and it is pasted among articles labeled March 1943 in Civil Defense Scrapbooks, WSA, ERB, Cheney. The letter-to-the-editor is not in microfilmed copies of the *Spokesman-Review* or the *Spokane Daily*

Chronicle, so the accuracy of the letter's publication information is uncertain; "Says Defense Lags; Publicity Is Needed," *Spokane Daily Chronicle*, 3 April 1943, 5; "Reeder Named Defense Chief," *Spokane Daily Chronicle*, 10 May 1943, 1; and "Strip the Civilian Council of Frills," *Spokane Daily Chronicle*, 16 November 1943, 5.

43 "Spokane Goes Wild Over News of Peace," *Spokesman-Review*, 15 August 1945, 1; and "All Quiet On Siren Front," *Spokesman-Review*, 14 August 1945, 6.

44 "Atomic Bomb Obliterates 60 Per Cent of Hiroshima City," *Spokesman-Review*, 8 August 1945, 1; and Editorial, "Terrifying Force Loose in World," *Spokesman-Review*, 8 August 1945, 4.

IV. Early Cold War Civil Defense Schemes, 1951–1958

45 "Teachers Called Pupil Guarders," *Spokesman-Review*, 8 December 1950, 6; Jim Kershner, *Carl Maxey: A Fighting Life* (Seattle: University of Washington Press, 2008), 87–89; "Bomb Shelter Check Planned," *Spokesman-Review*, 9 December 1950, 10; and "Dugger Urges Individuals to Cooperate in Defense," *Spokane Daily Chronicle*, 19 March 1953, 1.

46 Gerald R. Gallagher, "Introduction to the Symposium." In *Symposium on Human Problems in the Utilization of Fallout Shelters*, eds. George W. Baker, John H. Rohrer, and Mark J. Nearman (Washington, D.C.: National Academy of Sciences—National Research Council, 1960), 4–6; Guy Oakes, *The Imaginary War: Civil Defense and American Cold War Culture* (New York: Oxford University Press, 1994), 161; Eisenhower turned down other expensive public shelter proposals as well. Rose, *One Nation Underground*, 22; and Gallagher, "Introduction to the Symposium," in *Symposium on Human Problems*, ed. Baker, Rohrer, and Nearman, 4–6.

47 U.S. Executive Office of the President, National Security Resources Board, Civil Defense Office, *Survival Under Atomic Attack* (Washington, D.C.: U.S. Government Printing Office, 1950), 16; The distribution of the N.S.R.B. pamphlet is described in Oakes, *The Imaginary War*, 57; "River Banks Seen as Bomb Shelter," *Spokesman-Review*, 3 March 1951; City of Spokane Civil Defense Director Leighton L. Dugger reported to the Washington State Director of Civilian Defense that Spokane was considering the idea of riverbank shelters. Leighton L. Dugger to Philip D. Batson, 9 March 1951, Civil Defense Files, 03-A-416, box 5, folder: Spokane, City of, Correspondence 1950–59, WSA, SGA, Olympia.

48 "Duck and Cover," *Spokane Daily Chronicle*, 21 April 1952, 11; "25,000 Children Take Part in School Civil Defense Test," *Spokesman-Review*, 27 May 1954, 6; and "Defense Cartoon Is Recommended," *Spokane Daily Chronicle*, 18 April 1952, 1.

49 "Natural 'Safety Areas' Eyed in Air Defense," *Spokane Daily Chronicle*, 20 March 1953, 5; and "Buildings to Be Suggested as Downtown Raid Shelters," *Spokane Daily Chronicle*, 28 March 1953, 3.

50 Black residents of Spokane and black celebrity visitors such as singer Sammy Davis Jr. and jazz-great Louis Armstrong complained of businesses in the city that refused to serve black people. Jim Kershner, "Segregation in Spokane: Longtime Black Residents Recount the Injustices and the Victories," *Columbia: The Magazine of Northwest History* 14, no. 4 (Winter 2000–01); Kershner, *Carl Maxey*, 104, 109, 134; The template for a whites-only shelter was created in civil defense programs of the Southern United States. Andrew D. Grossman, *Neither Dead Nor Red: Civilian Defense and American Political Development During the Early Cold War* (New York: Routledge, 2001), 94.

51 "H-Bomb Odds: 1 Million to 1—And That's What May Save Us," *Newsweek*, 5 April 1954, 28, 33; "Big Defense Test Gets National

Spotlight," *Spokesman-Review*, 26 April 1954, 1; Spokane adds evidence to support historian Laura McEnaney's assertion that "local agencies enacted national policies." Laura McEnaney, *Civil Defense Begins at Home: Militarization Meets Everyday Life in the Fifties* (Princeton: Princeton University Press, 200), 8–9; and Department of Civil Defense, State of Washington, *Information Bulletin*, no. 85, 14 April 1954, 1, Civil Defense Files, 03-A-416, box 22, folder: Information Bulletins 1953–54, WSA, SGA, Olympia.

52 "Spokane Defense Walkout Called Success," *Spokesman-Review*, 27 April 1954, 1; "U.S. To Eye You Spokanites Told," *Spokesman-Review*, 24 April 1954, 1; "CD Leader Busy On Future Plan," *Spokesman-Review*, 28 April 1954, 6; John Balloch, et al., "Spokane Civil Defense Exercise 'Operation Walkout'," 26 April 1954, National Academy of Sciences, Committee on Disaster Studies, Washington, D.C., 3; "Operation Termed Success by City, State Officials," *Spokane Daily Chronicle*, 26 April 1954, 1; For a comparison of what such a crowd might have looked like as it paraded through the streets, consider Spokane's Bloomsday, the annual fun run held on the first Sunday of May, which its creator once described as "Woodstock on waffle soles." It would attract more than one thousand runners and walkers in its first year in 1977, more than five thousand in 1978, upwards of ten thousand in 1979, and by 1987, fifty thousand participants coursed through the city. Don Kardong, *Bloomsday: A City in Motion* (Spokane: Cowles Publishing Company, 1989), iii, 14, 80.

53 "Guard to Help Walkout Drill," *Spokane Daily Chronicle*, 23 April 1954, 3; "Thousands Evacuate Downtown Area in First Operation Walkout," *Spokesman-Review*, 27 April 1954, 22; "Varied Test-Alert Jobs Keep Thousands Busy During Operation Walkout," *Spokane Daily Chronicle*, 26 April 1954, 7; "Operation Termed Success by City, State Officials," *Spokane Daily Chronicle*, 26 April 1954, 1; "Guard to Help Walkout Drill," 3; "One Called It Operation Soakup," *Spokesman-*

Review, 27 April 1954, 6; Department of Civil Defense, State of Washington, *Information Bulletin*, no. 86, 30 April 1954, 2, Civil Defense Files, 03-A-416, box 22, folder: Information Bulletins 1953–54, WSA, SGA, Olympia; "Operation Termed Success by City, State Officials," 1; "Thousands Evacuate Downtown Area in First Operation Walkout," 22; and "Bombs, Guns to Add Realism to Walkout," *Spokane Daily Chronicle*, 23 April 1954, 3.

54 Federal Civil Defense Administration Public Affairs, "For Your Information: Hoegh Announces National Policy on Shelters," 7 May 1958, Civil Defense Files, 03-A-416, box 32, folder: Shelters, Public 1960–61, WSA, SGA, Olympia; "If Bomb Hits: Home Shelters Offer Chance." This article, without any specific publication information, was pasted into the November 1958 section of Civil Defense Scrapbooks, WSA, ERB, Cheney; "CD Evacuation Plans Dropped," *Spokane Daily Chronicle*, 20 November 1961, 2; "Civil Defenders Advised to Plan," *Spokesman-Review*, 19 March 1955, 1; "Civil Defense Situation in County Is Scrutinized," *Spokesman-Review*, 26 October 1962, 6; and "Series Praised," *Spokesman-Review*, 13 November 1961, 5.

V. Backyard Bunkers and Basement Hideaways, 1953–1962

55 Photograph, Civil Defense Files, 03-A-416, box 22, folder: Photographs 1956–61, WSA, SGA, Olympia; Federal Civil Defense Administration, *Facts About Fallout Protection*; "CD Denies Any Survey," *Spokane Daily Chronicle*, 25 August 1960, 5; "Civil Defense Inquiries Increase After Speech," *Spokesman-Review*, 27 July 1961, 6; and "Crisis Spurs Shelter Building," *Spokane Daily Chronicle*, 27 September 1961. This article was not found in microfilmed copies of the *Chronicle* but it was located, without any page number information, in Civil Defense Scrapbooks, WSA, ERB, Cheney.

56 Walter Karp, "When Bunkers Last in the Backyard Bloom'd," *American Heritage* 31, no. 2 (February/March 1980): 86.

57 "CD Office Says Business Brisk," *Spokane Daily Chronicle*, 24 August 1961, 18; "New Interest Being Shown in Shelters," *Spokesman-Review*, 1 September 1961, 1; and Podvig, *Russian Strategic Nuclear Forces*, 450, 444–445.

58 "Fallout Shelters," *Life*, 15 September 1961, 95–108; and "Mayor and Council Urge More Fallout Shelters," *Spokesman-Review*, 26 September 1961, 1.

59 "Shelter Move Taken," *Spokesman-Review*, 28 September 1961, 6; *Official Gazette of the City of Spokane, Washington* 51, no. 42, 21 October 1961, 537; "Shelters Increase; 26 Get Permits," *Spokane Daily Chronicle*, 8 November 1961, 1; and "Permits Needed for A-Shelters," *Spokane Daily Chronicle*, 13 October 1961, 3.

60 "Hints Offered: No Shelter Crooks in Region," *Spokane Daily Chronicle*, 29 November 1961, 13; and Joel Ream, "Fallout Shelter Building Boom Does Quiet Collapse," *Spokesman-Review*, 8 July 1962, 10.

61 McEnaney, *Civil Defense Begins at Home*, 64–65; Charles C. Ralls to Chet Holifield, 24 February 1960, Civil Defense Files, 03-A-416, box 32, folder: Shelters Public 1959–60, WSA, SGA, Olympia; "25 A-Fallout Shelters Estimated in Spokane," *Spokane Daily Chronicle*, 15 August 1960, 10; "Need Seen for Shelters," 25; and Don Rice, "Residents to Get Details on Nuclear Attack Safety," *Spokane Daily Chronicle*, 6 November 1969, 1.

62 "Home and Car Haven from Bomb If—," *Spokane Daily Chronicle*, 18 March 1953, 1; "CD Chief Urges Bomb Shelters for Spokanites," *Spokane Daily Chronicle*, 23 March 1953, 5; The test

Chaffins witnessed is described in Samuel Glasstone, ed., *The Effects of Nuclear Weapons* (Washington, D.C.: Government Printing Office, 1962), 200.

63 "Air-Raid-Minded Johnsons Offer Services and Shelter," *Spokane Daily Chronicle*, 27 March 1953, 3.

64 "Home Shelter Is Built," *Spokane Daily Chronicle*, 25 December 1958, 21.

65 "Shelter Eyed by CD Group," *Spokane Daily Chronicle*, 8 September 1960, 5.

66 *Wesley S. Wagoner v. Audubon Fuel, Inc.*, Spokane Superior Court, case number 2-162293, Spokane County Clerk's Office Archives Department, Civil Roll No. 1973, document 1, 7; "Shelter Trial Takes Recess," *Spokane Daily Chronicle*, 2 June 1961, 3; and "Oil-Soaking of Shelter Related in $9,600 Suit," *Spokesman-Review*, 2 June 1961, 10A.

67 "Crisis Spurs Shelter Building," *Spokane Daily Chronicle*, 27 September 1961. The article page number is not clear in the civil defense scrapbook and the news item is not among the microfilm copies of the *Spokane Daily Chronicle* held at Washington State University. Civil Defense Scrapbooks, WSA, ERB, Cheney.

68 "Bomb Shelter Has Periscope," 5; Kathleen O'Sullivan, "Ready for Fallout: Valley Family Has Shelter," *Spokesman-Review*, 5 March 1961, 10; Clyde J. Chaffins to Charles C. Ralls, 17 January 1961, Civil Defense Files, 03-A-416, box 32, folder: Shelters, Home 1961, WSA, SGA, Olympia.

69 The extent of the demonstration shelter program is mentioned in Karp, "When Bunkers Last Bloom'd," 86; and "Raid Shelter Contract Let," *Spokane Daily Chronicle*, 29 March 1960, 5.

70 "Atom Shelter Bid Is O.K.'d," *Spokesman-Review*, 29 March 1960, 7; "Work Planned on A-Shelter," *Spokane Daily Chronicle*, 12 March 1960, 1; The ground-breaking ceremony is pictured in Photograph, Civil Defense Files, 03-A-416, box 22, folder: Photographs 1956–61, WSA, SGA, Olympia; "Fall-Out Shelter Open to Public," *Spokesman-Review*, 25 May 1960, 6; and "War Experiences Told," *Spokane Daily Chronicle*, 19 February 1959, 23.

71 "Shelter Is Opened," *Spokane Daily Chronicle*, 24 May 1960, 5; The conditions for accepting one of the free shelters are explained in "Everett Fallout Shelter Will Be Opened With March 26th Ceremonies," *State of Washington Civil Defense Bulletin*, no. 51, 21 March 1960, 5, Civil Defense Files, 03-A-416, box 21, folder: Civil Defense Bulletins (Information Bulletins) 1958–60, WSA, SGA, Olympia; "Public Invited to See Shelter," *Spokane Daily Chronicle*, 23 May 1960, 1; "Raid Shelter Seen by 400," *Spokesman-Review*, 10 August 1960, 9; "Shelter Open," *Spokane Daily Chronicle*, 8 October 1960, 3; and "Fallout Shelter Proves Popular," *Spokane Daily Chronicle*, 2 October 1961, 3.

72 He also wondered, "If Americans are so concerned over survival, why do so few of them have seatbelts (at $10 a set) in their cars?" Denton R. Vander Poel, letter to the editor, *Spokesman-Review*, 10 November 1961, 4.

73 "Fallout Shelter Survey 'Phony'," *Spokane Daily Chronicle*, 9 October 1961, 1.

74 "Atomic Fallout Shelter Company Is Organized," *Spokesman-Review*, 16 October 1960, 29.

75 Ream, "Fallout Shelter Building Boom," 10.

76 Advertisement, *Spokesman-Review*, 13 September 1961, 3.

77 The shelter went to Maj. C. J. Agenbroad, who buried it in the yard of his family's home at West 1022 Beacon; "Costs Cut," *Spokane Daily Chronicle*, 13 September 1961, 36; Advertisement, *Spokane Daily Chronicle*, 20 November 1961, 2; Advertisement, *Spokane Daily Chronicle*, 30 January 1942, 14; "Fallout Shelters," *Spokane Daily Chronicle*, 27 October 1961, 18; Advertisement, *Spokane Daily Chronicle*, 9 November 1961, 47; and Ream, "Fallout Shelter Building Boom," 10.

78 Department of Defense Office of Civil Defense, *Personal and Family Survival: Civil Defense Adult Education Course Student Manual* (Washington, D.C.: U.S. Government Printing Office, 1966), 64; Ream, "Fallout Shelter Building Boom," 10; and Advertisement, *Spokesman-Review*, 26 October 1962, 12.

79 "Official Raps Shelter Ads," *Spokane Daily Chronicle*, 15 November 1961, 16; "Hints Offered," 13; and "Are You Confused? Shelter Talk Won't Help," *Spokesman-Review*, 19 November 1961, 19.

80 "Spokane Firms Busy; Fallout Shelter Business Booms," *Spokesman-Review*, 8 October 1961, 11; and Advertisement, *Spokesman-Review*, 12 November 1961, 8.

81 "Spokane Firms Busy," 11; and Advertisement, *Spokane Daily Chronicle*, 19 October 1961, 45.

82 Advertisement, *Spokesman-Review*, 22 October 1961, 10; Advertisement, *Spokane Daily Chronicle*, 3 November 1961, 15; Advertisement, *Spokane Daily Chronicle*, 7 November 1961, 22; and Advertisement, *Spokane Daily Chronicle*, 9 November 1961, 47.

83 Graybill, "Tales of a Shopping Bag."

84 Kelso, "Addresses Survival Meet Here," 10; "Atom Shelter Bid O.K.'d," 7; "Work Planned on A-Shelter," 1; O'Sullivan, "Ready for

Fallout," 10; and Charles C. Ralls to Gene Farinet, 20 October 1961, Civil Defense Files, 03-A-416, box 23, folder: Publicity 1961–69, WSA, SGA, Olympia.

85 Mrs. G. Miller, letter to the editor, *Spokesman-Review*, 1 May 1961, 4; and L. B. Knisley, letter to the editor, *Spokesman-Review*, 18 November 1961, 4.

86 Phillip W. Amborn to Senator Jackson, 4 May 1961, Henry M. Jackson Papers, Accession 3560-3, box 63, folder 9, Special Collections Library, University of Washington, Seattle.

87 Jack E. Fischer, "Heavily-Armed B-52s Are Ready," *Spokesman-Review*, 9 November 1961, 1; and "Sen. Jackson Sees Threat of Germ War: Says Expensive Shelters Could Erode U.S. Might," *Spokesman-Review*, 11 November 1961, 1.

88 Potter, letter to the editor, *Spokesman-Review*, 4; Lena Butler, letter to the editor, *Spokesman-Review*, 19 November 1961, 4; and Mrs. Walter Senters, letter to the editor, *Spokesman-Review*, 26 November 1961, 4.

89 The Sun Sales Corporation of Spokane declared that they were having trouble selling shelters, too. Ream, "Fallout Shelter Building Boom," 10.

90 "Interest Lagging in Bomb Shelters," *Spokesman-Review*, 6 May 1962, 2; For a quick survey of the nation-wide collapse of the shelter business see Karp, "When Bunkers Last Bloom'd," 93.

91 Ream, "Fallout Shelter Building Boom," 10.

VI. Public Fallout Shelters, 1961–1978

92 Frank Hewlett, "CD Director of Spokane Urges More Federal Aid," *Spokesman-Review*, 27 June 1963, 8; "Radio-TV Address of the President to the Nation from the White House," 22 October 1962, in Laurence Change and Peter Kornbluh, eds., *The Cuban Missile Crisis, 1962: A National Security Archive Documents Reader* (New York: New Press, 1992), 150; The range of the Soviet missiles in Cuba and the fear that the crisis could trip the superpowers into a wider war are covered in Ernest R. May and Philip D. Zelikow, eds., *The Kennedy Tapes: Inside the White House During the Cuban Missile Crisis* (Cambridge, Mass.: Belknap Press of Harvard University Press, 1998), 122, 97, 657; Missile bases in the Spokane area are described in Duane Colt Denfeld, "ICBM (Intercontinental Ballistic Missiles) in Washington State," *History Link* (July 2012) http://www.historylink.org/index.cfm?DisplayPage=output.cfm&file_id= 10158 (accessed December 5, 2013); Spokane's vulnerability to a Soviet attack directed over the North Pole is illustrated in George Creek, "If Spokane Were Bombed, Part One," *Spokesman-Review*, 24 October 1962, 7.

93 "Where's Nearest Air Raid Shelter' CD Office Asked," *Spokesman-Review*, 24 October 1962, 7; and "Home Defense Outlines," *Spokane Daily Chronicle*, 24 October 1962, 3.

94 The scope of the public shelter program is described in "CD Starts Survey of Shelter Sites," *Spokesman-Review*, 2 December 1961, 12. E. M. Llewellyn to Albert D. Rosellini, 30 September 1962, Civil Defense Files, 03-A-416, box 9, folder: Reports to Governor 1961–62, WSA, SGA, Olympia; and "Crisis Planning Pushed by CD," *Spokane Daily Chronicle*, 25 October 1962, 22.

95 May and Zelikow, *The Kennedy Tapes*, 339.

96 Ibid, 338–339.

97 Chang and Kornbluh, *The Cuban Missile Crisis*, 379–80; By October 29, 1962, Kennedy was ordering plaques to give to his advisors to commemorate their achievement in successfully handling the crisis. May and Zelikow, *The Kennedy Tapes*, 660–61.

98 Kerr, *Civil Defense in the U.S.*, 119–121; Rose, *One Nation Underground*, 37; C. G. Prahl to Walt Horan, 6 November 1961, Walt Horan Papers, cage 192, box 314, Manuscripts, Archives, and Special Collections, Washington State University, Pullman; The Northwest & Alaska Division of the U.S. Navy Bureau of Yards and Docks ran shelter surveys in 26 Washington counties. The Seattle District of the U.S. Army Corps of Engineers supervised shelter surveys in twelve Washington counties. The Walla Walla District of the U.S. Army Corps of Engineers oversaw the shelter survey of Walla Walla County. Charles C. Ralls to County, Metropolitan & Special Area Civil Defense Directors, 5 January 1962, Civil Defense Files, 03-A-416, box 32, folder: Shelters, Memoranda 1960–63, WSA, SGA, Olympia; and "Shelter-Site Survey Firm Chosen Here," *Spokane Daily Chronicle*, 19 October 1961, 19.

99 "A-Shelters for Public to Be Sought," *Spokesman-Review*, 14 December 1961, 6; "Shelter-Site Survey Firm," 19; Charles C. Ralls to County, Metropolitan & Special Area Civil Defense Directors, 5 January 1962, Civil Defense Files, 03-A-416, box 32, folder: Shelters, Memoranda 1960–63, WSA, SGA, Olympia; and State of Washington Department of Civil Defense, *Information Bulletin*, no. 169, June–July 1964, 4, Civil Defense Files, 03-A-416, box 21, folder: Civil Defense Bulletins (Informational Bulletins) 1961–65, WSA, SGA, Olympia.

100 "A-Shelters for Public," 6.

101 U.S. Office of Civil and Defense Mobilization, *Fallout Shelter Surveys: Guide for Architects and Engineers* (Washington, D.C.: U.S. Government Printing Office, 1960), 23–52; and Department of Defense, Office of Civil Defense, Region 8, Everett, Washington, "This document contains questions and answers which concern the National Shelter Survey Program," 5 January 1962, 3–4, Civil Defense Files, 03-A-416, box 32, folder: Shelters, Memoranda 1960–63, WSA, SGA, Olympia. Hereafter reffered to as DOD, OCD, "Questions and Answers," Civil Defense Files, 03-A-416, WSA, SGA, Olympia.

102 "Defense Shelters Found for 382,900," *Spokane Daily Chronicle*, 5 October 1962, 3; "Shelters Contain Limited Supplies," *Spokane Daily Chronicle*, 20 August 1964, 39; "Supplies Set for Shelter," *Spokesman-Review*, 20 December 1967, 7; Spokane City Plan Commission and U.S. Army Corps of Engineers, *Community Shelter Plan*. DOD, OCD, "Questions and Answers," 1, Civil Defense Files, 03-A-416, WSA, SGA, Olympia; and Hewlett, "CD Director of Spokane," 8.

103 DOD, OCD, "Questions and Answers," 12, 1, Civil Defense Files, 03-A-416, WSA, SGA, Olympia; and Department of Defense, Office of Civil Defense, "Statistics for Third Quarter of Fiscal Year 1970," *Information Bulletin*, no 242, 24 June 1970, Civil Defense Files, 03-A-416, box 21, folder: Defense Department, Office of Civil Defense Information Bulletins 1963–70, WSA, SGA, Olympia.

104 "Headquarters Hit on CD Supply-Lack," with a handwritten notation "SC 4-29-63" is in Civil Defense Scrapbooks, WSA, ERB, Cheney, but was not found in microfilmed copies of the *Spokane Daily Chronicle* or the *Spokesman-Review* available at Washington State University Library, Pullman; "Spokane Lags: State Stocking Shelters," *Spokane Daily Chronicle*, 27 April 1963, 7; "Civil Defense Supplies Here," *Spokane Daily Chronicle*, 7 May 1963, 1; and "City CD Facilities Ready, Supplies Stocked," *Spokane Daily Chronicle*, 5 November 1963, 20.

105 "Shelters Contain Limited Supplies," 39; "Emergency Security," *Spokesman-Review*, 7 January 1965, 5; and "Civil Defense Shelters Set for Population," *Spokane Daily Chronicle*, 1 March 1967, 5.

106 Department of Defense, Office of Civil Defense, *Fallout Protection: What To Know and Do About Nuclear Attack* (Washington, D.C.: U.S. Government Printing Office, 1961), 32; Robert S. McNamara, "Statement of Secretary of Defense Robert S. McNamara Before the Military Operations Subcommittee of the House Committee on Government Operations," 1 August 1961, Record Group No. 77 U.S. Corps of Engineers Walla Walla District Organization Plans and Publication Record Sets 1953–1970, box 22, folder: 250/17 Gen (1961) Emergency Planning Files-Fallout Shelter Survey-COFF 31 Dec 61, FRT RHA Jun 63, National Archives-Pacific Alaska Region, Seattle; and Federal Civil Defense Administration, *Facts About Fallout Protection*, 32.

107 "No Shipments: Shelter Stocks to Stay Here," *Spokane Daily Chronicle*, 17 December 1974, 5; "Officials Here to Ignore Survival Biscuit Order," *Spokane Daily Chronicle*, 8 January 1977, 20; "Viet Nam War Not Pushing Interest in Civil Defense," *Spokane Daily Chronicle*, 29 June 1965, 29; "Officials Here to Ignore," 20; Don Rice, "Shelter 'Ordeal' for Some, Fun for Others," *Spokane Daily Chronicle*, 13 March 1967, 1; "Increasing Interest Seen in Civil Defense Shelter Programs," *Spokane Daily Chronicle*, 3 April 1967, 13; and "Shelter Fare Tasted," Civil Defense Scrapbooks, WSA, ERB, Cheney. The article, with the handwritten notation "5-13-63," had no other publication information and can not be found in microfilm copies of the *Spokesman-Review* and the *Spokane Daily Chronicle* held at the Washington State University Library, Pullman.

108 Department of Defense, Office of Civil Defense, *Instructions for Filling the Civil Defense Water-Storage Container* (Washington, D.C.:

U.S. Government Printing Office, 1962), 2, Warren Magnuson Papers, Accession 3181-4, box 130, folder 21, Special Collections Library, University of Washington, Seattle.

109 Department of Defense, Office of Civil Defense, *Fallout Protection*, 37; and State of Washington Department of Civil Defense, *Information Bulletin*, no. 163, April–May 1962, 5, Civil Defense Files, 03-A-416, box 21, folder: Civil Defense Bulletins (Information Bulletins) 1961–65, WSA, SGA, Olympia.

110 "Shelters Contain Limited Supplies," 39.

111 Department of Defense, Office of Civil Defense, and Department of Health, Education, & Welfare Public Health Service, *Fallout Shelter Medical Kit Instructions*, 1962, 3–4, 8. The author found these medical instructions inside a box labeled "Medical Kit C: Survival Supplies Furnished by Office of Civil Defense Department of Defense." The box was stacked among abandoned fallout shelter supplies in the furnace room of Jackson Heights High School in Holton, Kansas.

112 "Bibles Added to Civil Defense Equipment," *Spokesman-Review*, 18 February 1965, 6; "Flags for Fallout Shelters Given City," *Spokesman-Review*, 22 October 1967, 10; and "Honor Earned by VFW Post," *Spokane Daily Chronicle*, 16 February 1968, 3.

113 State of Washington Department of Civil Defense, "Fact Sheet," 17 May 1962, 4, 5. Department of Civil Defense, Administrative Subject Files, Accession 03-A-416, box 20, folder: Women's Activities 1962–63, Washington State Archives, State Government Archives, Olympia; "Need Seen for Shelters," 25; By March 31, 1970, the national public fallout shelter program had succeeded in marking 109,470 structures in the United States with public fallout shelter signs. Department of Defense, Office of Civil Defense, "Statistics for Third Quarter of Fiscal Year 1970," *Information Bulletin*, no 242, 24 June 1970,

Washington State Department of Civil Defense, Administrative Subject Files, Accession 03-A-416, box 21, folder: Defense Department, Office of Civil Defense Information Bulletins 1963–70, Washington State Archives, State Government Archives, Olympia.

114 John Calcaterra, "Volunteers Asked for Shelter Test," *Spokane Daily Chronicle*, 18 February 1967, 1; John J. Calcaterra, "CD Volunteers Enter Isolation," *Spokane Daily Chronicle*, 11 March 1967, 1; and Rice, "Shelter 'Ordeal' for Some," 1.

115 Advertisement, *Spokane Daily Chronicle*, 3 November 1961, 15; and Cross Reference Sheet, "Shelters," 31 October 1961, Civil Defense Files, 03-A-416, box 32, folder: Shelters, Home 1961, WSA, SGA, Olympia.

116 John H. Rohrer, "Impications for Fallout Shelter Living from Studies of Submarine Habitability and Adjustment to Polar Isolation," in *Symposium on Human Problems*, ed. Baker, Rohrer, and Nearman, 24; and Delbert C. Miller, "Some Implications for Shelter Living Based on a Study of Isolated Radar Bases," in *Symposium on Human Problems*, ed. Baker, Rohrer, and Nearman, 53–54.

117 Executive Office of the President, Office of Civil and Defense Mobilization, "Pittsburgh Study Concludes Two-Week Shelter Stay Shows No Serious Effects," *Information Bulletin*, no. 287, 14 March 1961, Civil Defense Files, 03-A-416, box 32, folder: Shelters, Public 1960–61, WSA, SGA, Olympia.

118 "Management for Shelters Course Topic," *Spokane Daily Chronicle*, 24 February 1964, 3; Newspaper accounts did not make it clear how many of these managers were volunteers from the ranks of city employees and how many were sprouted from the general public. "Shelter Managers Are Badly Needed," *Spokesman-Review*, 25 March 1964, 5.

119 Calcaterra, "CD Volunteers Enter Isolation," 1; Rice, "Shelter 'Ordeal' for Some," 1; and "First CD Fallout Test Ends for 78," *Spokesman-Review*, 13 March 1967; 1.

120 Brad Smith, "Smith Lives Through Destructive Nuclear Blast," *Gonzagan*, Gonzagan Preparatory School, Spokane, 25 March 1967, 2.

121 Rice, "Shelter 'Ordeal' for Some," 1.

122 Smith, "Smith Lives Through Blast," 2; and Rice, "Shelter 'Ordeal' for Some," 1.

123 Smith, "Smith Lives Through Blast," 2 and Rice, "Shelter 'Ordeal' for Some," 1.

124 "First CD Fallout Test Ends for 78," 1.

125 Calcaterra, "CD Volunteers Enter Isolation," 1.

126 Shaun O'L. Higgins and Laura B. Lee, eds., *Ice Storm '96: Days of Darkness, Days of Cold: A Pictorial Record of the Worst Winter Storm in the History of the Inland Northwest* (Spokane: New Media Ventures, 1996), 70, 74, 84–85.

127 "Increasing Interest Seen," 13.

128 "County Area Shelter Maps to Be Mailed," *Spokesman-Review*, 7 November 1969, 2e; "Shelter Plan Copies Go Out," *Spokane Daily Chronicle*, 12 November 1969, 43; "Shelter Plan Mailing Ends for County," *Spokesman-Review*, 21 November 1969, 14; Wayne Carlson, "Civil Defense Prepared for Nuclear Attack," *Spokane Daily Chronicle*, 28 November 1968, 79; and Spokane City Plan Commission and U.S. Army Corps of Engineers, *Community Shelter Plan*.

129 Department of Defense, Office of Civil Defense, "Community Shelter Messages Go To 48 Million People," *Information Bulletin*, no 245, 29 September 1970, Civil Defense Files, 03-A-416, box 21, folder: Defense Department-Office of Civil Defense Information Bulletins 1963–70, WSA, SGA, Olympia; "Shelter Program Readied," *Spokane Daily Chronicle*, 3 February 1967, 5; According to the *Spokesman-Review*, the Policy Advisory Council was "composed of mayors of all the towns in the county, citizens, and a county commissioner." The composition of the Technical Committee was not detailed in the *Spokesman-Review* or the *Spokane Daily Chronicle*, but the credits in the *Community Shelter Plan* revealed that the civil defense directors for Spokane and Spokane County and two medical doctors were among the twenty-eight-person group. "Shelter Plan Will Be Aired July 31," *Spokesman-Review*, 16 July 1967, 6; Spokane City Plan Commission and U.S. Army Corps of Engineers, *Community Shelter Plan*; and Rice, "Residents to Get Details," 1.

130 Ibid.

131 "Shelter Program Readied," 5.

132 "Interest in Civil Defense Picks Up in Spokane," *Spokane Daily Chronicle*, 24 July 1967, 11.

133 "Shelter Policy Unit Suggests Time Change," *Spokane Daily Chronicle*, 20 November 1967, 8; and Spokane City Plan Commission and U.S. Army Corps of Engineers, *Community Shelter Plan*.

134 Dick Gentry, "Missile Crisis Over But Fallout Shelters Remain Stocked Should Public Need Them," *Spokane Daily Chronicle*, 18 December 1976, 5.

135 "Thieves Loot CD Depot," *Spokane Daily Chronicle*, 18 February 1964, 6; John W. McConnell to All State and Local Civil Defense Directors, 10 November 1966, Civil Defense Files, 03-A-416, box 21,

folder: Defense Department, Office of Civil Defense Information Bulletins 1965–68, WSA, SGA, Olympia; "Break-Ins Cited: Shelters Lose Sedatives," *Spokane Daily Chronicle*, 1 October 1971, 5; and "CD Kits Have No Sedatives," *Spokesman-Review*, 6 October 1971, 6.

136 DOD, OCD, "Questions and Answers," 11, Civil Defense Files, 03-A-416, WSA, SGA, Olympia.

137 "Wheat Wafers Planned as Food for Shelters," *Spokesman-Review*, 16 December 1961, 12; "No Shipments: Shelter Stocks to Stay Here," *Spokane Daily Chronicle*, 17 December 1974, 5; "Official Here Ignore Survival Biscuit Order," *Spokane Daily Chronicle*, 8 January 1977, 20; and "Survival Crackers Not Destroyed Yet," *Spokesman-Review*, 4 February 1977, 18.

138 Michael Lipsky, "Things Fall Apart: Problems of Governance and Social Control," in *The Counterfeit Ark: Crisis Relocation for Nuclear War*, eds. Jennifer Leaning and Langley Keyes (Cambridge, Mass.: Ballinger Publishing, 1984), 148; Margot A. Henriksen, *Dr. Strangelove's America: Society and Culture in the Atomic Age* (Berkeley: University of California Press, 1997), 305; Edward H. Judge and John W. Langdon, *The Cold War: A History Through Documents* (Upper Saddle River, New Jersey: Prentice Hall, 1999), 128–129; Kennedy ratified the test ban treaty on October 7, 1963. "Nuclear Testing Banned," *Spokane Daily Chronicle*, 7 October 1963, 1; Historian Paul Boyer wrote that the 1963 treaty led to "a sharp decline in culturally expressed engagement with the issue" of nuclear war and civil defense. Paul Boyer, *By the Bomb's Early Light: American Thought and Culture at the Dawn of the Atomic Age* (New York: Panthenon, 1985, reprint, Chapel Hill: University of North Carolina Press, 1994), 355.

139 Kerr, *Civil Defense in the U.S.*, 132; Boyer, *By the Bomb's Early Light*, 359; and "Viet Nam War," 29.

140 Steuart L. Pittman, "Afterward," *Who Speaks for Civil Defense?*, ed. Eugene P. Wigner (New York: Charles Scribner's Sons, 1968), 112; and John E. Davis, "From the Director's Desk," *National Association of State Civil Defense Directors Report*, December 1970, 3, Civil Defense Files, 03-A-416, box 5, folder: National Association of Civil Defense Directors 1967–71, WSA, SGA, Olympia.

141 Jack E. Fischer, "Heavily-Armed B-52s Are Ready," 1; Rose, *One Nation Underground*, 204; and U.S. General Accounting Office, *Activities and Status of Civil Defense in the United States: Report to the Congress by the Comptroller General of the United States, October 26, 1971*, 23, 19.

142 Swigard, "Civil Defense Fights Apathy," 1.

143 Editorial, "Civil Defense," *Spokesman-Review*, 17 February 1971, 4; and "Suggestions Made on Civil Defense," *Spokane Daily Chronicle*, 21 October 1971, 5.

144 Spokane, Wash., *"An ordinance changing the name of the Civil Defense Department of the City of Spokane to Emergency Services Department," Ordinance No. C21448* (1972); "Siren Test Cut Back by Council," *Spokesman-Review*, 30 May 1973, 1; "Fire Interest Surprises," *Spokane Daily Chronicle*, 18 September 1973, 3; and Youngs, *The Fair and the Falls*, 299–300.

145 B. Wayne Blanchard, *American Civil Defense 1945–1984: The Evolution of Programs and Policies* (Washington, D.C.: U.S. Government Printing Office, 1989) 17, 19, 21; and Editorial, "Civil Defense Unpopular," *Spokesman-Review*, 5 December 1978, 4.

146 "Evacuation Plan Drawn," *Spokane Daily Chronicle*, 7 March 1978, 3; and Jim Spoerhase, "Relocation Plan in Final Stages," *Spokane Daily Chronicle*, 17 January 1979, 3.

147 An item about the shelter signs appeared in a news roundup column whose main topic was animal cruelty. Steve Johnston, "Just Ask Johnston: Squishing Critters Isn't A Legal Issue," *Seattle Times*, 9 November 1998, http://community.seattletimes.nwsource.com/archive/?date=19981109&slug=2782602 (accessed May 13, 2009).

Conclusion

148 Dan Hansen, "Cold War Hideaway," *Spokesman-Review*, 28 April 1995, B1.

Made in the USA
San Bernardino, CA
12 February 2016